Portland Commun W9-CUA-660

I Know Fractions by Their Actions!

Tracy Kompelien

Consulting Editors, Diane Craig, M.A./Reading Specialist
and Susan Kosel, M.A. Education

Portland Community College

Published by ABDO Publishing Company, 4940 Viking Drive, Edina, Minnesota 55435.

Printed in the United States.

Credits
Edited by: Pam Price
Curriculum Coordinator: Nancy Tuminelly
Cover and Interior Design and Production: Mighty Media
Photo Credits: ShutterStock, Wewerka Photography

Library of Congress Cataloging-in-Publication Data

Kompelien, Tracy, 1975-
  I know fractions by their actions! / Tracy Kompelien
  p. cm. -- (Math made fun)
  ISBN 10 1-59928-529-0 (hardcover)
  ISBN 10 1-59928-530-4 (paperback)

  ISBN 13 978-1-59928-529-0 (hardcover)
  ISBN 13 978-1-59928-530-6 (paperback)
  1. Fractions--Juvenile literature. I. Title. II. Series.

QA117.K66 2007
513.2'6--dc22

                                                        2006012561

SandCastle Level: Transitional

SandCastle™ books are created by a professional team of educators, reading specialists, and content developers around five essential components—phonemic awareness, phonics, vocabulary, text comprehension, and fluency—to assist young readers as they develop reading skills and strategies and increase their general knowledge. All books are written, reviewed, and leveled for guided reading, early reading intervention, and Accelerated Reader® programs for use in shared, guided, and independent reading and writing activities to support a balanced approach to literacy instruction. The SandCastle™ series has four levels that correspond to early literacy development. The levels help teachers and parents select appropriate books for young readers.

Emerging Readers
(no flags)

Beginning Readers
(1 flag)

Transitional Readers
(2 flags)

Fluent Readers
(3 flags)

These levels are meant only as a guide. All levels are subject to change.

A fraction
names part of a whole.

Words used to talk
about fractions:
equal
half
quarter
third
whole

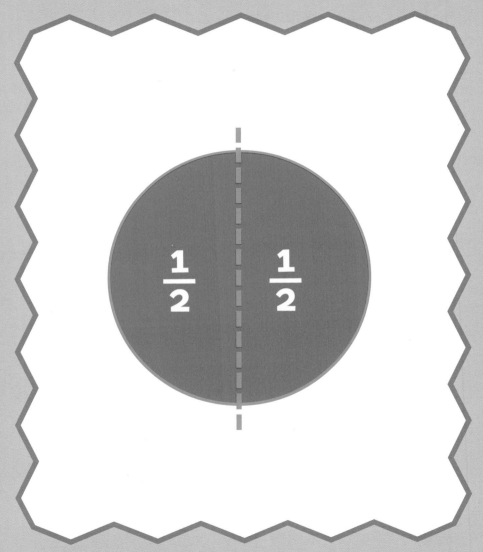

This circle has two equal parts. Each part is one half.

I know that two equal parts is the same as two halves, or the fraction $\frac{2}{2}$.

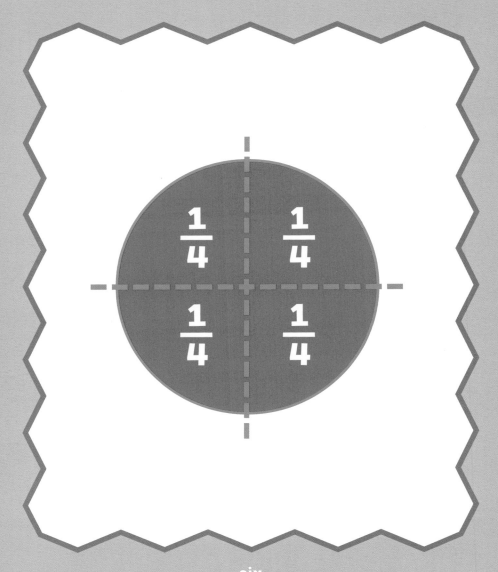

This circle has four equal parts.

I know that four equal parts is the same as four quarters, or the fraction $\frac{4}{4}$.

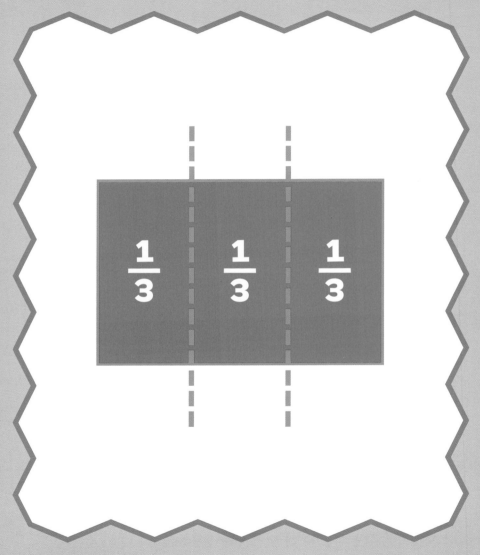

This rectangle has three equal parts, which are called thirds.

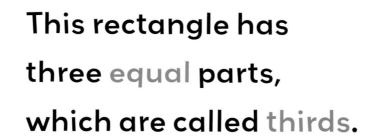

I know that three equal parts is the same as thirds, or the fraction $\frac{3}{3}$.

I Know Fractions by Their Actions!

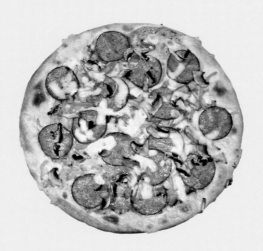

Frank has a pizza, and it is whole.

Whole means the entire object, 1, or $\frac{1}{1}$.

Frank has a laugh as he cuts the pizza in half.

Half means the object is split into 2, or is $\frac{2}{2}$. If I ate half of this pizza, I would be eating $\frac{1}{2}$ of the pizza.

fourteen

14

Two more friends want some of the order. Frank cuts it in four, and they each have a quarter.

I know that I should cut the pizza into 4 sections for 4 people. One of the sections would be $\frac{1}{4}$.

Using Fractions Every Day!

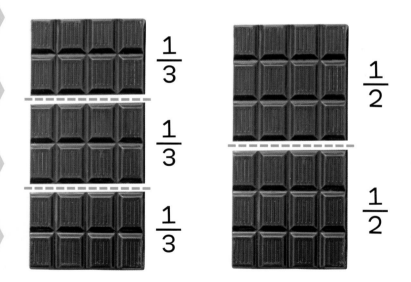

$\frac{1}{3}$

$\frac{1}{3}$

$\frac{1}{3}$

$\frac{1}{2}$

$\frac{1}{2}$

$\frac{1}{3}$ of a  is not as much as $\frac{1}{2}$ of a is.

If I split a chocolate bar with one friend, I would have more candy than if I were to split it with two friends.

eighteen
18

There is 1 .

Francy split the apple

in . She will eat

$\frac{1}{2}$ of the apple.

I know this because there is one apple split into two parts. This means there are two halves.

twenty
20

Francy split the  into 4 parts. She will eat $\frac{1}{4}$ of the after dinner.

The pie is split into four parts. I will have $\frac{1}{4}$ of the pie, which I also call a quarter or a fourth.

twenty-two

22

Think about what foods you like to share with your friends. What fractions do you use?

Glossary

equal – having exactly the same size or amount.

half – one of two equal parts. Half can be written as the fraction $\frac{1}{2}$.

quarter – one of four equal parts. Quarter can be written as the fraction $\frac{1}{4}$.

split – to separate or cut apart.

third – one of three equal parts. Third can be written as the fraction $\frac{1}{3}$.

he say,

she say

he say,

she say

Yolanda Joe

DOUBLEDAY NEW YORK LONDON TORONTO SYDNEY AUCKLAND

PUBLISHED BY DOUBLEDAY

a division of Bantam Doubleday Dell Publishing Group, Inc.

1540 Broadway, New York, New York 10036

DOUBLEDAY and the portrayal of an anchor with a dolphin
are trademarks of Doubleday, a division of
Bantam Doubleday Dell Publishing Group, Inc.

Design by Bonni Leon-Berman

Library of Congress Cataloging-in-Publication Data

Joe, Yolanda.
    He say, she say / by Yolanda Joe. — 1st ed.
      p.   cm.
    1. Man-woman relationships—United States—Fiction. 2. Young
women—United States—Fiction. 3. Afro-American women—Fiction.
I. Title.
PS3560.O242H4   1996
813'.54—dc20   96-2711
                                                        CIP

ISBN 0-385-48507-7

For my sister Donna . . .

who is smart, sensitive, and strong.

First . . . thanks to God, from whom all blessings flow.

Thanks to my family for their love and support, especially my mother, Carolyn, and my grandmother Bernice.

Thanks to my editor, Janet Hill, for her faith and her enthusiasm for my work.

A huge thank-you to my friends Val, Martina, and Francis for reading my manuscript and making suggestions that have made this book better.

Thanks to my agent, Victoria Sanders, for her support, hard work, and fun-loving attitude.

And last, but never least, thanks to the readers for supporting my work and having confidence in a new writer.

All the best . . . Love y'all . . . Yo

People who touch each other's lives create a circle of faith. When there is a crack it bleeds emotion.

s a n d r a   m a e   a t k i n s

sandy

I'm twenty-five years old and I'm actually *worried* about finding a good man to share my life with. Isn't that scary? Me, Sandra Mae Atkins, college-educated with a good sales job and just a quarter of a century old and yes, I'm already very concerned. Either society, my peers, or personal experiences—hey, maybe all three—have started me worrying about the quality and the future of my romantic life.

Last week I turned on the television and one channel told me that most of the men in prison are African American. I switched channels and the talk show's subject was: "My Man Is Cheating on Me with a White Woman."

I cut the television off and called my mama, who was happily married to my father until the day he died, and she said, "Times have changed. There just aren't any good men out there like your father anymore baby."

Is that pressure or what?

I think about the guys who have been in and out of my life. It makes me dizzy with disappointment. I feel like the world is telling me not to expect much but I want the best because I deserve it, don't I? I deserve love, attention, pampering, respect, happiness, and a meeting of the minds. I do! My mama had it.

I can remember my daddy being dark and handsome with long pretty lashes that fluttered over his large eyes. He was a construction worker and one of my earliest memories is of going downtown to the Loop to a site where a big building was being built.

Chicago was booming; putting up both office and apartment buildings. This particular site was on La Salle Street because I remember passing City Hall and the flags looked funny, all flying half the way down the pole. I remember Mama telling me in a hushed voice, "Sandy, that's a sign of respect. Mayor Daley just died."

I remember I fell back on the seat so I could see nothing but sky, buildings, and flags. Mayor Daley had visited our school once. I felt sad for his kids. And the idea of not having a daddy scared me. I was glad I was going to see mine.

When we got to the construction site, I remember thinking what a dirty and dangerous place my daddy worked in! There were mud puddles everywhere and dirt swirling in the air. All the workers had on jean overalls like I wore but theirs were thicker and a lot dirtier than I ever dared to get mine. And trucks were loud and driving crazy all over the place and there were no stop signs in sight. There were saws with big silver teeth and Daddy was in the middle of it all. He was using a machine with a silver fist to beat up the ground, punching holes in the mud. Mama and I honked the horn and Daddy's eyes smiled because I couldn't see his mouth, it was covered by a smudged white hanky, but his eyes? Yes, his eyes smiled at us for sure. Daddy came over to our car and took the slices of cake we brought for him and his friends.

Later that evening Daddy came home and I just knew he was going to be dead-tired and stinky. But he came in with all this energy and a big smile. And he didn't even smell *that bad*. I knew after I played in the sandbox and was sweating and jumping double Dutch that I stunk real bad. And Daddy had flowers. He had a big bunch of flowers for Mama and a little bunch of flowers for me! Mama gave him a big long, sloppy kiss. I thought she'd kill him because it didn't look like my daddy could breathe!

But Daddy came up for air and said, "Sandy, don't you want to go out and play for a while?"

Mama left no question. "Hurry up and go outside and play."

This memory is no fluke. Together, Mama and Daddy had it going on! Isn't that the way it's supposed to be?

So my expectations are high and I don't want to lower my standards. Why? Because that's not fair to me. I'm a searcher and a hoper. I guess that's why I'm so anxious as I sit around my apartment tonight just hoping and waiting. I met someone today.

I'm trying not to think about him but my mind and heart just won't cooperate. I'm just sitting here looking out of my apartment window. I'm trying to think about anything and everything except *him* and that *dang* clock.

11:05 P.M.

That clock is ticking hard, loud, and turtle-slow. Why is it time creeps when you're *not* having fun? Skip the clock. Skip him. It's a night so gorgeous I'd bet money that God sat back, blew a kiss, and opals and diamonds just sprayed out across the sky. On a night like this, so smooth and dark and sparkling, why can't I concentrate on that? Concentrate on something good and clean and magnificent like the beautiful evening sky? Oh no. Not me. Instead, my mind just keeps skipping a beat back to him.

In the opal of the night sky I see creamy jet-black skin spread over his high cheekbones, square jaw, and long, firm hands. In the sparkling sky I see the perfection of his gleaming smile and the light from his big, brown eyes. He sat regally in his chair and when he did get up, the movement was as fluid as a kite riding the wind. But back to . . . those . . . hands. His hands were big, soft, and luscious. The palms looked like—like what? I'm forced to say silk. Ye-s-s-s-s, silk. And his wrists? Superthick! His fingers fluttered across the piano keys—he was playing an original jazz piece—and as the music began to build, his fingers stretched and swelled and he jerked and pounded and caressed those keys. He raised his right hand and on the tip of his index finger was a drop of sweat that dripped onto the key of F-sharp, which was just lying there waiting for his stroke. When I was a little girl, I wanted to be Diana Ross or Iman. This was truly the first time I ever wanted to be a piano key. The song he played was mournful yet spirited, alive but shy, and it just ran all through me and slow-dragged at the base of my spine. I mean I wanted to *holler* in a room full of people—a room full of suit-and-tie sales and advertising folks in the radio business. We were on the third floor of our office in the banquet room for the quarterly sales party. And I *still* wanted to holler. No doubt everyone would have thought that I'd either lost my mind, was excited over my new promotion, was having a heart attack, or was in love at first sight.

11:18 P.M.

At the party I had tried to be cool. I heard the voice of my best friend, Bebe (she was going to come to the party but at the last minute had to cancel because she had to study for her night college class), and stayed put and didn't go rushing over to congratulate him like the rest of the women did. Bebe's raspy voice came just as clear to me. She's got this raspy tide of a voice.

I heard Bebe say, "Hold tight, girl. Let the stampede go by. You wait and stroll on through. Give him the eye. The look. Then stroll away and wait. He'll come."

All that is easy for Bebe because she approaches men like men usually approach women—as a conquest. Really, I don't know how she does it. But I waited. And waited. Those women just kept hanging around and hanging around. I mean they weren't budging.

So I ended up talking mostly to my boss, Harvey Dardin, thanking him for the promotion from sales rep to supervising sales rep. I would keep my clients and still do sales but I would also help supervise the production staff and help with the budget. It's a small station and Harvey created the position just for me. He was talking on and on. But it was hard to concentrate on Harvey despite the great things he was saying about me.

"You're a hard worker, Sandy," Harvey said. "You're my rising star, and I'll do all I can to help you."

But all I kept dwelling on was the song I had just heard. I was looking at Harvey and his high-arching hair weave. He'd seen the television commercials—believed and been deceived. But what a contrast. Fifteen feet away was a gorgeous man with glistening jet-black hair. Right next to me, Harvey rocked forward and while he talked, little balls of spit collected in the corners of his mouth. Across the room, *he* was standing looking suave-A cool. Harvey's great-grandfather owned the first jazz radio station in the city and he was in the business, well, because it was a family thing—nothing more. Across the room, there was this struggling jazz pianist who obviously adored every note a piano spoke and was trying to get his big break in the music industry.

Harvey did get my attention when he asked about my ex-boy-friend Dominique. I'd brought him to a few company events and everyone thought he was so charming. A charming snake is what he was, but I wasn't about to go into it then, and I won't go into it now. I can't talk about it just yet. Harvey is so nosy! And men say *we* gossip.

Harvey asked, "What happened?"

I said, "Let's just say that trust was not there. There has to be trust between a man and a woman for any kind of relationship to work."

11:35 P.M.

Will he keep his promise? I'll know in just about twenty-five minutes. What will I know? I'll know whether or not T.J. Willet Jazz Pianist is a man of his word or if he is perpetrating like so many other brothers out there.

two

beatrice   mae   thomas

bebe

Sandy is my ace-boon-coon. My homette. But sometimes . . .
ooh-wee! Sometimes Sandy falls in love entirely too fast. Wham!
Sandy's in love. I was supposed to go to the sales party at her job
tonight but after I got off work at the bank I was so tired I decided I'd better go to the library right then or I wouldn't be going
at all! I'm trying to sew up this degree, and I only have a few
more months to go for my bachelor's in business. Then, hey-hey,
it's thank-you-Lordy as I step across that stage and do my Patti
LaBelle strut to get my diploma. Sandy said she wouldn't miss my
graduation for the world, but that she will just *die* if I do that
strut. Sandy said you're supposed to walk dignified and she proceeded to show me how she did it when she got her B.A. That
girl can make me smile! Look like Sandy stretched that five-foot-
two-inch body an entire foot higher. She concentrated as serious
as you please and marched a straight line with that stutter-step
walk. But whose degree is it? I will have earned it and it'll be
mine, and I'll get it how I wanna get it! Well . . . I don't know.
Maybe I won't as a favor to Sandy. She's like a little sister to me.
You know she's the one who encouraged me—no, bugged the hell
out of me—to go back to school to get my degree in business.
Period. All bows go to Sandy, because I was satisfied with my
high school diploma.

But don't get it wrong. I wasn't so uninspired as it seems. See, I
was fifth in Hyde Park High's Class of 1973. Make no mistake,
Beatrice Mae Thomas is and never was no dummy. I'm sharp, I

just didn't go to college! That's the only thing I truly regret in my entire forty-one years. I just loved money and wanted to make some so I could get my own crib. Living at home was more than my nerves could stand back then.

Mama and Daddy argued entirely too much for me. It was some fierce fightin' going on up in apartment 313, yes siree! It hurt my spirit. My heart. But Mama took it, though. All those years of harsh words and heavy licks. God, there was one time I never will forget. Daddy reached back and socked her. I mean Daddy tried to knock the stew out of her. And Mama? My mama? She took that lick like Joe Frazier in his prime. Sally Marie Thomas from Mount Bayou, Mississippi, did not shed nary a tear or move nary an inch. She was a stake driven into the ground. Later, after Daddy left, after I had cried all the juice out of my eyes, I asked. I had to ask Mama a question, and it took a lot of nerve for a ten-year-old to do that. You know back then you'd get your butt whupped for getting into grown folks' business. Not like now. So it took some courage but I asked Mama why.

"Why?" I said. "Why do you let him do you like that?" And do you know what she said?

Mama said, "Because I love him more than life."

Ain't that powerful? I'm not loving anyone that hard, and I'm sure not taking any licks. That's why I got out as soon as I could and started working at the bank. I also do tax work on the side and that brings in money. I have a rule: Uncle Sam is the only man I give money to. So I'm pretty comfortable, keep good money. But after I convinced Sandy to let me do her taxes and got her twelve hundred dollars back and that white guy only got her five hundred the year before, Sandy raved about me.

"Bebe," she said, "you're wasting your talent! You've got a sharp brain! You can do and have more! Get off your black ass and go back to school!"

Hold it now, I added that last part. Sandy doesn't talk like

7

that. Me? I'm regular. Now, don't be confused, I'm not common. Just regular. Regular as in cool with everyone; as in easygoing and no airs. That's old Bebe, just regular.

Sandy and I have this fun thing we do. I'll call up and sound really hurt, like moaning, you know, "San-day!"

She'll answer all excited, "Bebe!"

"San-day, call a doctor, girl!"

"What's wrong, Bebe?"

"Girl, we so fine it's killing me!"

And then together we'll both go: "Fine, fine as blackberry wine fresh off a California grapevine."

Then we'll both just crack up laughing.

We did it tonight, as a matter of fact, when I called to ask how the party went. Sandy couldn't wait to tell me about this man she met. Some piano player. I tried to picture him from Sandy's description and he sounded like a Slo Poke—long, lean, and chocolate all over. Gorgeous was Sandy's word.

"He's stunning," she said.

"A fine motherfucker," I said.

Sandy said, "Right."

Then Sandy started tripping on his hands. Now, Sandy has this thing, and I try to let people be who they are. I believe that your ways are simply your ways. Never, ever try to change anyone. But Sandy has this thing where she just gets, daydreamy? No, uh, poetic is more like it. Now, I appreciate things like that. I mean when Maya Angelou was at that podium reading her poem at Clinton's inauguration, I cried revival meeting tears because I was so moved and so proud. So I do appreciate vision. But Sandy was tripping on the man's hands trying to draw a connection with his manhood, if you dig where I'm coming from.

"You know what they say about big hands, Bebe," she said.

I played the nut roll. "What, Sandy?"

That threw her. Then Sandy said really mean through the phone, "You know. I know you know!"

8

I said, "Well, he was sitting at the piano, right?"

And Sandy said, "Yeah."

"So instead of all that fantasizing why not check it out?" Boy! What did I say that for? Sandy just went nuts!

"Bebe!" she said. "That's so tacky!"

Now I was hurt. I mean check it out, as in cut your eyes. You might be able to figure out what the game will be—golf or baseball. I mean, he was sitting there and every man I know sits with his legs cocked wide open, it would have been very easy to sneak a peek. What's the harm? I'll answer my own question: none. I didn't say *go there*. Just cut your eyes on the sly. Shoot, men check us out up and down, every whichaway. They stare at our breasts, our hips, our legs, our ass. And men will be just as bold as you please about it. That calmed Sandy down a little bit because as I said before I'm not common, just regular. And a regular sister would have been suave-A about checking it out. I mean what was tacky—sneaking a peek or Sandy sitting by the phone for four hours waiting on him to call?

"You've been sitting by the phone waiting for four hours?" I asked her. Sandy said she hadn't done anything! No bubble bath. Didn't oil her hair. No cable. No reading. Nothing. And I said, "Sandy!"

Then she said softly, "Well . . . I . . . I . . . He . . . promised."

And Sandy sounded so disappointed I was hurt for her. I hate when men do that. Don't take a number and say you're gonna call and you're not interested. Period. Just go on. I didn't know T.L. or J.L. or whatever his name was but he had disappointed my friend, and I was about to start talking about his mama, his daddy, and his dog, who I was gonna name Newt. Then Sandy's call waiting kicked in, she clicked over, then back, and said all excitedly that it was him.

"T.L.?" I said.

"T.J.," she said, snapping my head off. "I'll talk to you later."

I looked at the clock, 11:58. And I must say I was impressed.

three

timothy james willet, jr.
t.j.

I almost didn't call Sandy. After I left J-108's party I went over to
the Pelican to play a happy-hour set there. Between the two
places I must have collected four phone numbers. Two ugly
chicks sat right in my face at the Pelican and what one had the
other one didn't. The dark one was overweight by thirty pounds,
the light one needed the thirty, plus two. The dark one needed a
perm and the light one's hair was falling out. The dark one had
braces and the light one needed a set. And they had the nerve to
send over a napkin with *both* their phone numbers on it. I took it
and smiled and kept playing and then when they weren't looking,
I wiped the sweat off my forehead with it.

Now I was down to two phone numbers from the J-108 party.
One was written on a business card and the other was on a flyer
that advertised the company that had catered the party. The
number on the flyer belonged to the first lady to rush over to me
after my little set at J-108. Ladies were crowding all around me
cooing my performance. I played like a master. There was power
in my stroke and emotion behind it too. I just wish I could capture that in the studio. But for some reason, every time I try to
record, the power just doesn't come through. The juice is gone.
Zap! It's as if some demon erases it and I can't find it anywhere.

Anyway, not only had I played well at that party, I looked
damn good too. I had on my black Italian suit that hung loose at
the shoulders and tapered in at the waist. Armani shirt. Armani
tie. C.K. cologne. I had generously dabbed some behind my ears

10

and on the tips of my fingers, so when I caressed a lady's face she got a subtle whiff.

And Tia? She was the first one over to me and I lightly touched her face. I felt a strong physical attraction between us. I could tell by her flirting that she felt it too. Tia had a fabulous body. Big luscious breasts. Pencil-thin waist. Brick-house butt. Barry Bonds could hit fifty homers with her legs. She was the first woman on me and I let her be. I could feel her firm nipples against my arm as she rubbed up against me. *All* the girls were in my fan club except one who stood over in the corner talking to some old white guy. When Tia brought back my drink, I asked her who he was and she said the boss. The girl, Tia said, was just sucking up to him like she always did at the job.

"Everyone is talking about it," Tia said. "That's how she got promoted."

So Tia's number was the first one that I called after I finished at the Pelican. She said, "I live near, stop by."

I stopped to buy some condoms and then I took a cab over. Tia had a nice apartment—but her colors were too dark, cobalt blues and grays. Tia tried to hold a conversation with me but it was very awkward. I asked her about the mayoral election that was coming up, asked her if she was a Democrat or a Republican. No joke, Tia said some stupid stuff.

She said, "I don't vote because it doesn't make a difference anyway. African Americans will always get the short end of the stick."

Then I asked her what she thought about my song and she said something about it being pretty. Pretty? Ding-dong, everybody. She had a brick-house body with no electricity on upstairs. The only other I.Q. I wanted to find out about was her Intimacy Quiver. One thing was for sure: Tia was not relationship material at all. But I wasn't going to leave without tasting that fabulous body.

The first thing I did was drench Tia with compliments—real and imaginary ones—because all women like to be made to feel special. Then I hit the light and took her into my arms. She didn't struggle and she didn't protest my forcefulness, they almost never do. I gave her hard kisses and stroked her ear with the tip of my tongue. Her blouse unbuttoned down the back. I ran both my hands across the back of her head, down to her shoulders to caress her back, then I played the buttons like a scale and flicked them loose. Tia asked me about condoms and I told her that I believed in a safety net for sure. She said she was on the Pill. Cool, so I put my stuff on.

Then Tia whispered in my ear, "Bedroom?"

I was so swollen at that point I didn't want to move. So hey, I whispered back, "Right here on the floor."

Before Tia could answer I slid her right down, peeled off her panties, and laid my stuff right between her breasts. I let it sit there and throb and I told her softly, "Taste it."

And she did. Her mouth had heat I imagined a comet would have. I felt my head spinning and I grabbed her breasts and held on. Then I eased back and let my dick blaze a trail down the middle of her body and I delicately entered her and gathered steam as our desire began to build. It was too quick for me and I wanted more. But Tia couldn't hang and I could tell she was through.

I thanked her for the good love with a soft kiss. Then I looked up at the clock and it said 11:50. I was supposed to meet my dad at his hangout at 12:30 and I'd promised a phone call to what's-her-name, the lady who hung back and who I approached just before I left the J-108 party. I excused myself and took my pants and headed for the bathroom. I passed the cordless phone and picked it up without Tia seeing. I didn't want to hurt her feelings or disrespect her in her own home. I tiptoed into the bathroom and closed the door.

I looked in the mirror. My face was moist with sweat and my eyes were a little tired from such a long day—practice, the free lessons I taught at the community center, the performance at the radio party, the set at the Pelican, and now this. I smiled, pleased with the fact that I still had energy to burn and I wasn't worn out. I guess I got my juice from the old man—after all, I was a Jr.

Anyway, I grabbed some toilet tissue and cleaned myself up before slipping on my underwear, then my slacks. I grabbed a tube of toothpaste out of the cabinet and squeezed a dab onto my index finger and scrubbed my teeth with it. I ran the cold water, cupped some into my mouth, swished it around, and spit it out. Then I ran the warm water and got a dab of liquid soap and washed my face. I let the water drip down from my forehead onto my broad nose, over my top lip, and down over my chin. I dried my face with some Kleenex, got the phone number out of my pocket, and sat on the edge of the old-fashioned tub and looked down at its claw feet. I fingered the phone antenna and read the number and name I had.

Sandy. There was something about Sandy that I liked. She wasn't beautiful but she had an attractive face. There was something about her eyes, big and expressive. And she had long lashes too. It wasn't a pretty face but a classy, strong face that you would remember. She carried herself with class and had good taste in clothes—she was wearing an Anne Klein suit that fit her well. She didn't have a booming body; in fact, she was a bit on the skinny side. But she wore her clothes well and there was just something about her. I liked the fact that she didn't crowd me like the other women even though I could look in her eyes and tell that she wanted to. I caught her looking my way a couple of times while she was talking to her boss. Sandy seemed to have a little game about herself and I liked that. Before I left I decided to go over and talk to her for a minute. I took the empty glass out of her hand and stroked the inside of her wrist with my index finger and said, "I'm T.J. What would you like to taste?"

And she answered, "I'm Sandy and I'll like whatever you bring me."

I went to the bar and brought her back white wine and she asked, "Where's yours?"

And I said, "I'm looking at all I thirst for right now."

I thought she would fall out. I whispered in her ear, "Give me your number and I'll ring you."

And Sandy answered back, "When?"

And I said, "Before the day is gone."

I thought a few more minutes and reminded myself to talk low so Tia wouldn't hear, then I dialed Sandy's number.

four

sandy

"Hello, it's me."

That's just what T.J. said and I know I should have said me who? but he sounded so good. T.J. sounded so good with his deep, sexy voice. I said back to him, very softly, "You're a man of your word."

And T.J. said, "Yeah, I try to be. A man should keep his word. Trust is very important between a man and a woman."

Oh God, I wanted to reach through the phone and hug him. That's what I always say. I say that! And here he was saying the same thing! Is that too much? This could be the beginning of something, I could feel it already! After Dominique, I needed someone, someone to restore my faith in relationships. I really, really, *real*—lly wanted to believe him as he talked about how I'd captured his attention. I knew he wasn't lying because he remembered the suit I had on and the fact that I didn't drink much at all. So I felt comfortable admitting that I had watched him too. I asked him what "T.J." stood for and he said, "Timothy Jr."

So I said, assuming, "Then everyone calls your father Timothy."

And he said, "No, everyone calls my father Speed."

"Speed?" I laughed.

T.J. said, "Yeah, because he used to be a train conductor. And since you asked, that reminds me that I have to go and meet Daddy."

And I must have sounded sad when I said, "Oh." As soon as it came out I wanted to choke myself! I had to sound like a lonely

15

chick! I tried to rebound by adding, "Oh, it's getting late for me too."

T.J. went on to say how he promised his dad he would stop by and see him. T.J. said, "Me and Dad are very close, more like brothers than father and son."

I thought that was really nice. I mean you don't hear about a lot of fathers and sons who are that close and that's really special nowadays. I was liking this T.J. more and more. In my mind I chanted, Ask me out. Ask me out. I started saying it faster and faster and faster. Ask me out. Ask me out.

And T.J. said, "Sandy!"

I was hoping so hard that I zoned out. Finally I answered easily though my heart raced, "Yes, T.J.?"

And T.J. said it. "I want to see you again."

Now my breath was a little short and I told myself to calm down. So all I managed to say was, "O-kay."

And he said, "What about next week?"

Next week! Oh no, that was not going to work for me! I didn't want to sound pushy or anxious, but I *was* anxious and I wanted to be pushy, so I thought quickly, Bebe says I think fast on my feet. I said, "Why don't we have lunch tomorrow? Instead of the station mailing your check for the performance, I'll pull a few strings. I'll have it ready for you around lunchtime and we can grab a bite, how's that?"

T.J. said, "About what time are you talking?"

"Noon?"

And he said, "Hmmmmm." Hmmmmm is what he said and I just hung on edge until that last m sound got lost in space.

Then T.J. said, "I'll make it . . . just for you. Let's meet at Arturo's on Kinzie. See you soon."

I cradled that receiver against my chest and wondered why I was so hot to be with this man. Was I that hurt and lonely after Dominique? Or was he just about the sexiest man that I'd ever seen and I needed sexy and I wanted sexy and I just was dying to be with sexy?

I was a little scared that I was so excited and that I felt so strongly so fast. That's a danger I think for women. We feel so deeply and so fiercely so quickly. I was determined to savor this excitement but not sanctify it. I savored it and savored it. I thought of his gorgeous smile and his style and I savored and savored. Then the phone rang. I picked up and said, "Bebe girl." But there was no answer. Must have been a wrong number. So I savored the good feeling I was having and dozed on off to sleep. I'd call Bebe first thing in the morning.

timothy   james   willet,   sr.
speed

I was copping a squat at my table in the Players Lounge. I'd been at Players for two hours digging on the blues band, the Windy City Breeze. They played some shit for your ass! They got this sax man that makes that horn sound like a moaning hound dog! The sound gets so low-down you can't even stand up straight. I swear your knees will just buckle. I'm a fun-loving man and I believe in enjoying good music, good food, and good people. I like to have a good time. Man, I'm like this—men and women should enjoy each other, that's why we were put here together, for company's sake.

I spotted this young girl in the corner, swinging to the groove. I could tell she was a dancer and since I like to step, I decided it would be fun to hook up with her. I gently took her hand and asked, "May I have this dance?"

It was on from there! I ain't lying we was jamming. We got two or three good bump-and-grind dances in. This young thang had titties like bullets and thighs like submarines. Her dress was supertight, clearly two sizes too small. I could tell she was looking for a sponsor. Her shoes were run over, the leather on the heels had stripped back like a banana peel. Her dress was out of season, too thin for Chicago's switchblade wind. Shoot, that wind starts whipping off the lake and it'll cut you to shreds! This girl needed on some heavier clothes! I thought that maybe she had just run over in the car and had only been outside for a few seconds. Nope. 'Cause then I noticed she had a food coupon and a bus token mixed up with her change on the bar counter. She was a very public person; living on public aid and riding public transportation. But Sweet Jesus, she was sexy; big brown eyes and nice skin. She had the widest mouth I'd ever seen on a woman. I was hugging her hips with my hands and we had a blue-lights-in-the-basement bump and grind going on in the corner of the room. See, I had nodded to the D.J. who was spinning records between sets. Blood put on my favorite album by the O'Jays and played a cut called "Stairway to Heaven."

Hey now! I was humming the record and grinding our stuff together, humming and grinding. Humming and grinding. Got the rhythm? If somebody hada put some dough between us we coulda rolled out sliced bread. I didn't even sing 'til near the end when I went for that high note! And out of the corner of my eye, in the reflection of the cymbals I saw it coming.

Blam! Claaaaaaa-nnnnng!

I broke away from her just as some dude swung a bottle at me. It came crashing down against that cymbal and it jumped up and cried the blues all by itself. *Claaaaaaa-nnnnng!* Hear what I'm sayin'? The cymbal knocked two drinks over. Glass flew in the air like gnats flying. But he missed. Big mistake.

I cupped my fists and threw a one-two punch from the hips, knees bent—I'd been a damn Golden Glove boxer in my day. And here somebody was trying to take me out with a bottle? And for what? I didn't even know the dude! Man, I threw those punches—*pah-pow!* and *bam!* That nigger was out of season like watermelon at Christmas. He was a big joker too. His feet reached almost to the bar and his chest was as big as the drum section he was knocked out against. I looked at my dance partner, stunned, and I remembered that I hadn't even asked her name.

"Who the fuck is he, lady?" I asked her. And she hesitated because she was shaken up, excited by the whole thing. I touched her arm and said, "Calm down. Nobody is gonna hurt you. Who is he?"

By now the crowd was gathering in close. She started fanning herself with an open napkin and said, "He's my ex."

I said, "Ex what? Ex-husband? Ex-boyfriend? Ex-stalker?"

She said, "My ex-husband."

Now the owner, my partner, a retired cop named Outlaw Jack, came busting through. I said real cool, "Man, sorry about this. He had a bottle and . . ."

Then Outlaw threw up his hand and grabbed a pitcher of water off the bar and doused it in the dude's face. Outlaw reached down, slapped him twice, and said, "Hey! Hey!" Then Outlaw shouted over his shoulder, "What's his name?"

Somebody in the crowd yelled out, "Ace."

I had to laugh. An ace is tops in the deck. An ace is sharp and can't be beat. This young buck went out like a deuce—head hit, feet hit—one two!

When Ace woke up, Outlaw grabbed him by the neck and said loud enough for everybody, "I don't like nobody trying to tear up what's mine. I was a cop on the street for thirty years and ain't a motherfucker walking on earth, in hell, or in the clouds that scares me. I will not have a whole bunch of mess in my place." Outlaw pointed down. "Ace, don't try me. I'll break your neck in five places and the rest of the places will jump scared and break on their own! You better get out of my club. And take your lady with you. Both of you are banned from Players."

She turned and looked at me and I touched Outlaw on the arm and gave him a nod. Outlaw caught my meaning right away. He said, "The lady can stay if there's no more problem."

I winked at my boy. The last thing this woman needed was to be thrown outside with this hothead. I enjoyed watching Outlaw throw Ace out. Ace's eyes got big and he slobbered, "What about him?"

Outlaw said real downlike, "Everybody know me and Speed go way back. I know Speed ain't start no mess in my place. He's with me. Me and Speed is partners." Outlaw was giving me my props. Then he said, "Now break it up everybody, the next set will begin in twenty minutes."

I bought the young lady a drink and asked her if she had a way home. She said she would have her drink and then be on her way.

I proceeded to head back over to my spot. I brushed the glass off of my blue suit and looked for cut places. I paid two hundred dollars for the suit. Luckily, it was still okay. No snags in the fabric. No stains from the whiskey that was left in the bottle. My blue wing-tip shoes were still shining and I stepped on back to my table.

I heard clapping coming from the corner booth. I heard clapping from the Witches Brew. That's what me and Outlaw jokingly called them. They were four women and they all used to look fine! Me and Outlaw both had done the do with a couple of them but now they had let themselves go and that was a damn shame for fine women to just give up like that. A fine woman should never give up on herself but hey, I would still flirt with them anyway because they all had a place in my heart for old time sake. I bowed to the Witches Brew and sent over some drinks.

Ann yelled out and held up her beer. "Thanks, Speed! You still can knock 'em out!"

I held my glass back up, smiled, and drank it down. I motioned for the barmaid to send me over another drink. I got it and chugged down that Crown Royal before chasing after it with a sip of Miller. My heart was beating but I had to look cool. There was a tightness like somebody was sitting on my chest. I eased air in and out of my throat until I had calmed down. It wasn't fear. Nope, wasn't fear. I had an irregular ticker and my doctor had told me to cool it, take it easy, and I was trying. That was one of the reasons I took early retirement from the railroad. So I sat there, my leg across my thigh, my hand on my ankle, the other hand on my drink, looking cool but feeling a time bomb ticking inside. I leaned back in my chair and glanced around the bar.

There was always a nice crowd in Players even on a weeknight. It was a nice-sized place too; nice big bar in the center and delicate tables on the side for two folks to talk. There were booths too, not too high so a man could watch his back and a lady could see the show real clear. Yep-yep-yep, a bunch of places that was stone-to-the-bone tough in the sixties and seventies had gone down but not Players. Players Lounge still had class 'cause it still had its regulars like me and, well, also 'cause Outlaw wasn't going to let it go down. I sat there for a while and then my son showed up.

"What's up, Daddy?" T.J. said, and his smile instantly calmed me down. He just had that kind of power over me, T.J. did, my son.

I said, "You, Player." And we hugged and slapped each other's back loud as all outdoors. He looked good. When I look at T.J., I see myself in my prime. He's built up like me, broad shoulders and tapering waist. Tall. Smooth. It's like God is giving me a chance to watch myself all over again in T.J. He's all class, that boy. Yep-yep-yep! Me and his mama made an outstanding baby, shoulda had more.

T.J. sat down across from me and threw up two fingers. That's his signal for a glass of champagne. Outlaw kept a couple of bottles of Moët for T.J. Didn't nobody in there really drink it but him. Anyway, when I caught that, 'cause usually he don't drink real late during the week, I leaned forward, sniffed real hard twice, and said, "Something smells good!"

T.J. sniffed and shrugged. "Cologne?"

I sniffed real hard again, looked around all confused, then got up and walked over to T.J., sniffed his collar, and joked, "Naw. Pussy."

We both cracked up. T.J. swayed back and around on the stool.

"Daddy," T.J. said, "I had her going. I was kissing her hard all on her neck and face and I sucked her breasts."

I cupped my hands to my chest.

"Twice that," T.J. whispered. "Man, she had giant nipples too."

"Big as bottle tops," I laughed. T.J. gave me that half-smile of his and a quick wink.

Then he cocked his head and said, "I was working her, Daddy."

"Stroking." I laughed again and called for another Crown Royal. "Did you get off?"

T.J. held up two fingers and I smiled! That boy was just like me! I asked him, though, "How come you didn't spend the night and get a little more in the morning?"

He said, "I'm a busy man, Daddy."

I said, "Naw, she was moaning so loud you didn't want the neighbors to call the police!" I threw out my left hand and T.J. threw out his right hand, we hooked index fingers, pulled back, and snapped our fingers. T.J. said he just wanted to stop by for a minute and then he was going home to work on a song he'd tried out earlier at the radio station party. I asked him how it went and T.J. said great, that that was where he met the girl he'd banged tonight. He met another girl there too. What'd T.J. say her name was? Sandy? Yeah. Seemed like I've known a Sandy or two in my lifetime. Always liked those Sandys. "Pretty?" I asked.

T.J. said, "Not really, but a face you'd remember. Classy."

"Oh," I said, "you might let this one hang around, huh?"

He reared back just like I do, then ran his hand over his chin and said, "Naw, I'm going to hit it and quit it."

We hooked fingers, pulled back, and snapped. That's my boy. That's my boy.

bebe

If someone asked, "Bebe, what would you change about yourself?" I'd tell them straight, "I'd love me some bouncing and behaving hair!" I mean it's seven in the morning and my hair is a mess! I'm combing and combing and the do just ain't doin'. I'm spraying this sheen stuff and it's doing a fabulous job fogging up my mirror but my hair is still out the box. I mean c'mon now! I asked Kay—Kay is my hairdresser—oh excuse me, hair*stylist*, though my hair is doing anything but styling—I asked her to give me a strong conditioner to tame these locks because this is ridiculous. I mean one part is headed east, the other part is headed west, and the middle is lost in space. My head is the final frontier. Okay, I'm exaggerating and it isn't that bad but I can't do anything with it and I've always been tender-headed. I'll never forget that one time when I was nine and my mama took me to Miss Peaches' Beauty Shop.

It was close to Easter and Mama had bought me this baby-blue satin dress with a big bow in back to wear. I'd seen it on television in one of those old Shirley Temple movies and I just cried and boo-hooed until Mama said she'd talk to Miss Cookie. See, Miss Cookie sewed by ear; tell her what you wanted and she would whip it out. She was a gifted seamstress and worked at a bridal shop on the North Side for some rich white folks.

I had the dress tucked under my arm and Mama marched me to Miss Peaches' Beauty Shop. As soon as I got there Miss Peaches took one look at my nappy pigtails and said, "Girl, why you let that chile walk around like that? You got good hair. But that chile needs a perm bad!"

Mama said quick as you please, "No chemicals, just press it."

Miss Peaches squatted on her bowlegs and rocked side to side with her hands folded across her potbelly and hollered really loud, "Go on now with that country stuff!"

Everybody in the shop turned around and stared at us. There were three ladies working in the back of the shop and they had customers getting the white stuff plastered all over their heads. It looked like the paste in my jar at school, seemed sticky like it too, but it smelled funny and was beginning to give me a headache.

Mama asked Miss Peaches, "It burn, don't it?"

"Sweet Jesus, yeah!" a lady yelled from the back. She was holding onto the chair with both hands, tapping the floor with both feet, and making snake sounds with her mouth.

Miss Peaches answered real loud, "Burn only if the person is slow about putting it on and taking it off."

Mama said, "Makes your hair fall out, don't it?"

"Yeah, if the person don't know what they're doing," Miss Peaches answered.

Mama said, "Un-huh, no telling what white folks is putting in that stuff." She said, "I know they experiments on Negroes 'cause I had an uncle in Tuskegee, Alabama, who got the nasty sickness and them doctors kept giving him stuff and he never did get better. To this very day my family believes they were doing something to him. So please, don't tell me what white folks won't do!" Mama walked over to the counter behind Miss Peaches and picked up one of the metal curling irons and said, "A colored lady came up with these here, so I *know* they all right, so press and curl my baby for Easter or I'll let my little money walk elsewhere."

Miss Peaches' nostrils blew back so hard I thought she would choke but she didn't. She just came around and picked me up with one arm. My feet were way off the floor and she bent over and picked up a two-by-four with her free hand. At first I thought she was going to bat me like a ball. Instead, Miss Peaches laid it across the chair and sat me on top of it. Then she put a checkered kitchen apron around my neck and struck a match and lit the stove iron that looked like a big black spider laid out on its back. It came to life, though, with that fire. The yellow flame with blue roots shot out and eased back and Miss Peaches put one of the metal combs on top of the stove to heat it. Mama said, "Go slow, she's real tender-headed."

I said, "Please?" and looked real sad at Miss Peaches, hoping for mercy.

Then Miss Peaches said, "Okay, but look, this ain't no plantation. I don't need no overseer—go'n and do some window shopping and come back in an hour and I'll be through—uh, on second thought make that two hours."

I was all excited and shouted, "When you come back, I'll have Shirley Temple curls!"

Everyone just laughed and Mama grinned and left. As soon as she left, one of the hairdressers in the back cut loose and said, "See, that's why I hate it when these country-butt women come up here on the train fetching them cardboard suitcases with red dirt 'tween they toes and nothing 'tween they ears. They think as soon as they hit concrete they know everything and don't know shit from Shinola!"

I don't know what it was but I got hot all over and I hopped out of that chair and spoke as bold as you please. "My mama ain't never walked nowhere barefoot and her feet ain't dirty neither and she twice as smart as you." Now, I said all this while standing in my Little Sally Walker stance before I added, "I ain't suppose to sass no grown folks but don't talk about my mama like that 'cause God don't like ugly and if you don't believe me go ask the preacher and check." By then I was crying and from what little I could see Miss Peaches was smiling.

She said, "This chile got spunk and I don't want nobody stirring up my chile, so y'all shut up and let me make my little colored Shirley Temple beautiful."

And dogged if she didn't lay my hair out! It smelled terrible with all that Glover's hair oil in it but my hair was fried, fried and laid to the side!

Boy, what I wouldn't do to bring Miss Peaches back to fix my hair on a regular basis! The phone rang. I could barely get the receiver out of the cradle before Sandy started singing, "*Be-beeeeeee! Girl, call the doctor!*"

"What's wrong?" I said.

"Girl, we so fine it's killing me."

Together we sang, "Fine, fine as blackberry wine fresh off the California grapevine!"

And we laughed, then I said, "What's up with Mr. Thang?"

"Now, Bebe, that's not necessarily why I was calling," Sandy said.

I told her, "Please tell that to somebody who thinks spandex is a glass cleaner."

We laughed and Sandy said, "I dreamed about him all night long. It was the way T.J.'s voice sounded when he said, 'Hello, it's me.'"

Stealing from the Isley Brothers, I thought, but I didn't say anything. Sandy said that she was going to meet him for lunch today after she got a friend to rush a cut on T.J.'s check for the office party. Now, I know she thinks this boy is Billy Dee, Blair Underwood, Wesley Snipes—no scratch that he can't be as sexy as Wesley—but you get my drift, but here she was calling in favors for him already? Sandy said she was going to make an impression on him. And when Sandy says "I'm going to," that means she can't be budged on the issue. Case closed. I still thought that it was too soon to be doing the boy favors. I mean she didn't even know if he could kiss or not! Office favors, at least at the bank, seemed too hard to come by to waste, to me.

Now, that's to Bebe. But hey, I let it go 'cause it was too early to start another fight. Wasn't I already losing the battle with my hair? So I just told her to call me after lunch.

"Wait," Sandy yelled.

"Girl, I got to go! How does it look if the supervisor comes in late?"

Then Sandy said, "But what should I wear?"

"Something sexy," I said. She said something about it being lunchtime, so I told her to go ahead and be boring then.

Sandy started whining, "Well, I was just hoping for a little guidance from my best friend but if you can't help me out, then, well, I guess I'll just go in here and try to figure out what to do *all* by myself."

Now, Sandy doesn't even like how I dress, okay? But I started thinking so I could leave my girl with a good feeling and get the hell off the phone. I was thinking the royal-blue knit dress she had bought at the March Madness sale last year, 50 percent off, don't you know. The dress was a beautiful color and fit just right, not too loose or too tight. Sandy could wear it to work but at lunchtime she could break out a royal-blue and gold scarf I bought her for Christmas and her gold, big-looped belt with matching earrings. She could play those with it to give it some pop without being too out the box. But Sandy doesn't like the way I dress, so I went around the back way. I said, "Go to your closet and let's look."

I heard her moving and humming. I like it when Sandy hums. That means she's feeling very good. I heard the hangers slap against each other. "What color might be nice but not too loud?" I asked.

"Hey," Sandy said, "how about my royal-blue dress?"

"Well," I said, giving her a little line, "nice but boring, yeah?"

"Yeah, kinda but what could I do?" she asked.

I started reeling my homette in. "Try that scarf I gave you for

Christmas." I could picture her with the phone cupped to her ear, the dress tucked under her chin, and the scarf lying across her neck. "Perfect, huh?" I said.

Sandy agreed but I still heard a little reservation in her voice. "Not jazzy enough?" I said. "Accessorize, girl!"

That was it. You can lead Sandy right where you want her to go most of the time and she'll think it was her own idea. She went for the belt and the earrings too. Case closed! Damn, I'm good.

t.j.

Arturo's is a cozy little place on Kinzie off Wells. The nearby el train running overhead is a little loud at times and the tracks can cast shadows on sunny days but it's worth dealing with it. The place just reopened a few months ago and I like to hang out at new places to sort of break them in.

I was sitting in a side booth facing the door watching the ladies stroll into the restaurant. I was sipping on my third vodka and tonic waiting on Sandy. I'd picked Arturo's because it always had a steady stream of honeys coming through. Good-looking women, great scenery, and it was African American–owned. Plus, it was far enough away from J-108 that most likely Sandy and I wouldn't run into Tia. I hadn't promised Tia anything. It should have been clear to her that it was just a one-night boot knocking, but sometimes women get tied up too fast and make something out of nothing. I don't believe in messy scenes and I don't believe in unnecessary conflict. If you don't get too close or too bold or too serious, you won't have those problems.

I opened the menu and glanced at the list.

Suddenly a voice said, "Hello, you cheap motherfucker."

When I looked up, *pow!* A pitcher of ice-cold water was being dashed in my face. I grabbed a napkin and coughed and snorted as water flooded my windpipe.

"Where's my money?" Mikki said, waving the pitcher. Before I could answer, Mikki started hitting me with it. I was blocking blows left and right and lucky for me the pitcher was plastic. I finally grabbed her arms and squeezed her wrists until she dropped the pitcher. I jerked her around and crisscrossed her arms in front of her body to restrain her.

She calmed down and I said in her ear, "Miss Mikki. Fine Mikki with your long hair, hazel eyes, keen features, and ugly, spoiled ways. I don't owe you a damn thing, Miss Mikki, and if you don't get out of here right now I'm going to launch your narrow ass right out that front door."

Mikki yelled, "You said you loved me!"

"What?" I answered back. "No, I said I loved hanging out with you."

She looked confused. Mikki said, "You said you would pay me back."

"No, I said I'd make it up to you."

I knew everyone was watching but she had gone too far and I knew Mikki and the only way to end it was like this. "Do you see how you've acted? Huh," I said, "like a crazy, hard-up bitch. You're suppose to be a black socialite, the daughter of a wealthy businessman!"

"That five thousand dollars," she hissed at me.

I hissed back at her, "If you want it, I'll give it to you when I can but you can't get what I don't have! Now, if you don't get out of here I'm sure as hell gonna call all the gossip columns. And how will Daddy Big Dollar like that, reading in the newspapers about his black china doll acting like a common nigger in a bar?"

That did it. The thought must have knocked her out because she fainted in my arms. I was stunned. Shocked. I grabbed Mikki by the waist and sat her in a chair. A waitress ran over with a menu and started fanning her. She gave me that black girl loosey-goosey-neck, eye-rolling routine. I reached in my pocket and pulled out a ten-spot and gave it to her after I saw Sandy standing at the door.

sandy

Some lady fainted! I walked into the bar and T.J. was helping a lady who had fainted! His face was soaking wet and I started over that way. But he handed a waitress some money and came and grabbed me by the arm and said, "Let's go."

"What happened?" I asked. He said that the lady had started choking on some food and he had given her the Heimlich maneuver. T.J. said after the food popped out, she just fainted in his arms. "How'd you get so wet?" I asked.

And T.J. said, "I'd gotten so excited that I just started sweating like crazy. So I went to the bathroom and doused myself with water to calm my nerves before coming back out and seeing about the woman. I've never been in a life-or-death situation like that before. I gave the waitress my last ten dollars and told her to put the lady in a cab." Then T.J. took a breath and added very softly, "It was too intense for me, then I saw you and I just wanted to get out of here. I didn't want you to get all upset too."

Wow, he'd gone through a real ordeal. And it was so thoughtful of T.J. to want to get us out of the bar. Who would want their first date in that kind of atmosphere? I wouldn't. I had never been to Arturo's before and I didn't realize it used to be the Chi-lite Bar and Grill, so that's why I was late getting there. After what T.J. had just been through I wanted to take him somewhere quiet and cozy. T.J. was leaning up against me, chest-to-shoulder, and I could feel his heart patting my arm. T.J. was following me like a little boy. I asked him, "What's the rest of your day like?"

He said, "I've got piano lessons at the Y." He hugged my shoulders in.

I squeezed his waist and said, "I'm supposed to meet a client later but I can reschedule that, then I just have to pick up my best friend after work. Let me make lunch. I've got plenty of food in the fridge, and right now I'm in the mood for something solid and home-cooked and I just don't want to hear no."

When we got to my apartment, I was so glad I had spent my weekend cleaning up. It was spotless and my tenth-floor view of Lake Michigan was spectacular. I told T.J. to have a seat and I went over to my bar tray and asked him what he would like to drink. T.J. was standing by the window just gazing out. He was biting his bottom lip and his eyes actually looked watery. I walked over and touched his shoulder. T.J. turned to me and gave me a very insincere grin and said, "I'm sorry, my mind is elsewhere."

I asked him, "Do you want me to call the restaurant and ask if that lady is okay?"

And T.J. grabbed my hand as I reached for the phone. He kissed the inside of my wrist and said to me softly, "No, I'm sure she's fine."

And then he told me that he was thinking about something else, someone else. And T.J. dropped my hand and walked away toward the couch and sat down. I sat next to him, feeling helpless that I couldn't seem to ease the anxiety on his face, and I looked at him and asked, "Can you share?"

And T.J. turned and stared at me for a long moment. "It might frighten you," he said.

That gave me a huge chill. It's when he said that that I realized my heart had led me where my brain would never go. Here I was in my apartment with this man who I'd only known for a day and he could do just about anything and I'd be hard-pressed to stop him. I'd never done that before. Why now? Why had I opened myself up and become so vulnerable, so quickly? Why did I feel so good with this T.J. and so good about him? I'm cautious! I'm guarded! And here this man had me all adither and I was playing shrink trying to get him to open up. He could be a freak or something. But there was something about T.J. that told me that wasn't the case but I couldn't help but feel worried. What could he say that would frighten me?

t.j.

I scared Sandy and I didn't mean to do that. I was just feeling out of sorts. The truth was that Mikki's fainting had put me in mind of my mother. I looked at Sandy and I felt that I could tell her. I just shut my eyes and told her that the fainting incident had put me in mind of my mom. Mom was always having these fainting spells because she suffered from a mental illness and eventually died from a brain aneurysm. I didn't really want to tell Sandy but that ugly scene in the restaurant brought the memories back. But why? Was it the two drinks? The strain from that nasty scene with Mikki in the bar? Or maybe it was that double stuff plus Sandy feeling all warm and cozy next to me on the couch? I didn't really want to get so personal so quickly but sometimes things come out when you really don't want them to. They come out and you don't have the energy or the will to stop them. I wanted to talk, so I told Sandy about a particular incident. And Sandy was there on the couch and her ear was just there waiting, so I told her about something that happened a long time ago.

I was a toddler and I remember Mom grabbing her hair and pulling like crazy because she was in so much pain. I couldn't have been more than three because I remember being really low to the ground and there was this blue and white rattle near my feet and I've got baby toes. I know that it's me, and my mom is leaning near an eight-track tape player, jiggling the tape trying to make it play right, and she just grabbed the back of her ear. It's like she caught a pain and wanted to pinch it to a halt right there and my dad says that I must of dreamt this because Mom never told him anything about it. But I know it really happened.

I remember Mama pulling at her hair and she had such beautiful, full hair because there was Crow on her mother's side and that ancestry flowed from her scalp and rested heavily on her shoulders. I remember her falling backwards, her apron with its little unicorns on it roped around her waist. Mama twisted back and forth on the floor holding her temples. She was whimpering and I could do nothing as I watched. I remember her reddish brown skin turning purple and she started pulling and pulling at her hair.

Then Mom reached up and grabbed a pair of sewing scissors and started to cut the hair away from around her ears. Tears were streaming down Mama's face. I remember seeing my baby toes balling up into little knots. I must have screamed although I don't remember hearing my voice. But I do remember Mama jerking around, dropping the scissors, and crawling toward me whimpering, "Baby, sweet baby, baby." And then my mother reached down toward me and the rattle disappeared and my toes disappeared and all I remember next is the white scalp on the sides of her head where she cut her hair. And that's all.

Sandy gave me compassion and understanding through her eyes and her touch as she ran the back of her hand against my cheek. I leaned forward and puckered my lips as wide as I could and gave Sandy a wet kiss on the neck. She moaned and began to nibble and kiss. It was going on, let me tell you.

ten

bebe

Where is that crazy child?

I said, "Sandy, can you meet me after work and take me to class because my car is on the bonks?"

"Sure," she said.

"I've got a big exam in my stats class and it ain't nothing to play with."

Now, that's plain, huh? I told her to pick me up at four. That way we could beat the five o'clock rush to the expressway and I'd make my class on time. That stats is a bitch. I need every minute of test time! I'm standing outside looking for that little red car of hers, hoping it will turn the corner soon. Five then ten minutes pass. I know she's all excited about J.L.—or T.L.? Whatever! But if I mess up this exam, I'm in deep trouble.

I'm walking with my head down trying to think whether I should leave or not when—*bam!* I run smack into this guy. I bounced back off his stomach and said, "Excuse me!"

And he said, "Bebe?"

I looked this man up and down. He's got on these flooding double-knit pants buckled below his juicy stomach. He's got a fat face covered mostly by a straggly beard, but I knew those eyes. He had nice big, superblack eyes.

"Bebe," he said, "it's me—Dap."

Dap?! Get out of here! I'd read in class once that no man is an island but Dap? He was close! Lord, Dap had gotten big! He looked like he'd eaten all the food in the fridge and the freezer, then scraped the frost off and made a snow cone! I leaned in real close at those eyes, yep, it was Dap all right! And when I leaned that close I got a big whiff of some p-funk. I leaned back and had to go, "Wheez!" Then I played it off like I was so glad to see him. "Wheez," I said again, "it's been a long time."

"Yeah," Dap said. "Ain't seen you since the old days in the neighborhood, huh?"

"Dap" was short for Dapper because his daddy was a tailor and kept the boy clean as the Board of Health when we were kids. He was tall and slim and wore his clothes like a champ. Every girl in the neighborhood and high school wanted to be seen with Dap. Girls would cut class to wait outside the music room waiting on Dap. He called his self playing the trumpet and it sounded like my gramps farting but Dap looked too fine holding a horn. Now, just look at him. Dap was just standing there holding a packet of newspapers and he caught a glimpse of pity in my eyes.

"Awww naw, it ain't like that," Dap said.

I spoke up, "Dap, you don't have to be ashamed because you sell *Street Wise*." Dap got mad-mad!

"I'm not a seller," he said. "I'm a distributor!"

I was stunned. Before I could figure out what to do, one of the girls in the bank came out. Kiki. She never took a lunch so she could leave a little early to pick up her son from school and bring him back until she got off work. He stayed in the lounge and did his homework. Kiki said, "Hey, Bebe, thought you were gone?"

I said, "No, my ride is late."

Kiki looked all strange at Dap.

He broke out, "Me and Bebe used to kick it."

The look on her face was utter shock, then it turned to a smirk. "Really," Kiki said, and grinned at me.

I wanted to crawl up under the mailbox.

Dap broke out, "Yeah, that's when there were black velvet posters with strong brothers and sisters on them. And we had blowout kits and blue lights in the basement and mercy, mercy, we used to dance up a storm, 'member, Be?"

And before I answered, Dap broke out with a boogie beat and started doing the feelie. That big old stomach was just rolling and his hands were flying up and down feeling the air. Kiki looked like she was going to bust out laughing. Now Dap was singing, "Get off oowee-ooweee-ooooh," and doing the bump with the light pole. Just having a good old time, okay?

Kiki was behind his back mouthing the words "Get it, girl" and gyrating her hips! I gave her this nasty look and she just covered her mouth with both hands and started walking away. Kiki was going to tell everybody at work. She was a chatterbox. Kiki would tell a light pole your business. Now Dap was moving close to me saying, " 'Member our slow dances?"

I threw out both hands and said, "Lord, please, Dap."

"Too much for ya, huh?" he said.

"You know it," I answered.

Then Dap got this really sneaky grin and said, "How about I meet you here tomorrow?"

"No!" I said.

"Well," he moaned, "I might be convinced to get scarce."

Then I got the message. I pulled out five dollars and said, "Why don't you just go on about your business?"

Dap looked at the five and said, "For twenty you'll never see me again."

And I held the five up higher in his face and said, "Take the five and if you come around this bank again I'll call the cops and have you arrested for loitering."

Dap snatched the five and said, "You always could get evil in a minute!"

Before I could say something back, Dap had the audacity to blow me a kiss! Yes he did! I was so through! Dap took that cash and broke camp. I was so embarrassed and now I was on the verge of being late for my test! I finally decided to call a cab. I didn't want to go back in the bank, so I jogged across the street to the little deli. There was a pay phone by the door and I wanted to watch out in case Sandy finally did show. I rang her house just for the hell of it but there was no answer. I called a cab, then slammed the phone down.

I turned around to go and I heard a news flash on the radio playing over the door. It was some reporter live on the expressway saying that there was a six-car pileup. Multiple injuries. A dozen ambulances were at the scene. Witnesses said a red car started it by slamming into the back of another vehicle. I kicked my anger to the curb and my heart just stopped. That's the way Sandy comes. She could be in that accident. She has a red car— maybe Sandy hit somebody. She could be in the middle of that mess, hurt or something, and here I was acting all crazy mad. My stomach started aching like when I went on the Screaming Wolf at Great America. I grabbed it and thought, Stop, stop, don't go there! Sandy is not in that accident. But what if she was in some hospital emergency room all alone? But she's not! She could be? Then I just walked outside and back to the corner to wait for the cab. I was toying with the idea of calling the nearest hospital just to check. I looked up and the cab turned the corner and who was racing alongside of it? Sandy!

She pulled up and honked the horn. I could have killed her. Here I'd been waiting all this time, then embarrassed by that crazy, blackmailing, homeless Funkateer, then worried to death by that dang news flash and she pulls up talking about "Hey, Bebe!" Oh but no. I walked over to the car and then I saw one of my regular customers, Bernadette. She's a waitress and always has a lot of coins to count and we're supposed to charge 1 percent to change it into paper money, but I don't charge her on the q.t. because she's a single mother and all. She waved at me and I told her, "Go see Angie and tell her I said to take care of you." Bernadette just stared at me and Sandy in the car but I didn't have time for anybody else's attitude. I slammed the car door shut and tried not to go off on Sandy.

she say

Miss Perky piped up, "Bebe, you won't believe my day."

I looked at her and there was this big old giant hickey on her neck! I hadn't seen a hickey like that since tenth grade. I just turned and looked straight out the window and igged her in the best way. Sandy asked, "What's wrong?"

"Nothing," I said.

sandy

Nothing? Please! I know Bebe like Alice knows Trixie. Like Wilma knows Betty. Like Oprah knows Gayle. I could tell by the way she was sitting that she was angry. Her knees were clamped together tight and her lips were all poked out. I know I left late but T.J.'s lips were so sweet. And I couldn't foresee that accident that would tie up traffic. What could I do? I was driving a Saturn, not Chitty Chitty Bang Bang.

I said, "Bebe, I'm sorry I'm late." Do you know she wouldn't even look at me?

She said, "Shut up and drive!"

So, like always, I'm the cool one. So I started driving and ignored Bebe right back. I wanted to tell her about the lady fainting in the bar, T.J. being so heroic going to her rescue, the lovely lunch that we had, and all the stuff that went on afterwards. But no, Bebe was just sitting there patting her feet against the floor. Then all of a sudden she started barking orders to turn left and go this way, all that kind of bossy stuff. She even told me to take a shortcut through the alley. In my new car? I hesitated and then just went on because I didn't want to get Bebe any more upset than she already was.

I reached and turned the radio on because I wanted to hear my spots. Between 3:00 and 7:00 P.M. was *Afternoon Drive,* and my clients paid big bucks for this airtime and I wanted to make sure their spots sounded good. Bebe leaned over and cut it off. I cut it back on. She cut it off.

"I'm trying to study for my exam," Bebe said, and made her mouth really ugly when she said it.

I said calmly, "Bebe, I need to check my spots, okay? So I'll turn it down real low and you just take a break and I'll take a break." She just stared at me but I saw a soft spot in those eyes and I turned the radio back on.

Apollo was the afternoon D.J. and he has this sexy voice—you know, deep and comfortable—even when he recorded my spot and said, "And now this message from Lexus International in Winnetka."

That was the spot I was listening for . . . But it was dead air! What happened to that spot? It'd taken me three months to convince this Lexus dealer to advertise on our station! He was an older white man and figured that a small black-oriented jazz station wouldn't have listeners who could afford a forty-thousand-or-more car. I wined and dined him. I showed him demographics that showed we had a decent share of the listening audience during *Afternoon Drive*. I took him to an event we sponsored at a jazz club near the upscale East Bank Club and there was a mixed audience, people stopped by from the club. He'd finally said he would buy some time for today and if it went well he'd open an account and have some other suburban dealers call me too. And now, no spots? What could have happened? I ordered them. I had listened to them myself. Why weren't they running? My pager went off. I checked the number and it was the Lexus dealer.

I heard Bebe say, "I know you're not stopping to make a call when you've already made me late."

I just turned and looked at her.

"He can wait," Bebe said.

She thought it was T.J.?! Bebe was just too bossy! I clenched my teeth and drove as fast as I could. I wanted that heifer out of my car.

t.j.

This is how the afternoon went. I'd gotten Sandy comfortable with me and I stepped to her on the couch. I laid some passionate, sloppy wet kisses on her neck and ears. I ran my tongue along the small part at the base of her throat, then rolled it down the middle of her exposed chest. I worked my hands along her hips and up her back. Her perfume was losing its scent and it had the faint smell of crushed roses. She was tasty and I just licked and sucked her neck until my tongue went dry. I was coming out of my pants when she bolted upright and said, "God, Be."

"Bee?!" I jerked back. "Where's the bee?"

And she laughed and I didn't appreciate her laughing at me, so I asked her what was so funny.

Sandy said, "Be is Bebe, my best friend. I've got to go pick her up from work and take her to school."

"Aww," I said, easing back to her, "let her take the bus."

"No," Sandy said, "I promised."

Now, to me that sounded kind of childish. Here Sandy was with me and she wanted to rush off in the middle of the good thing we had going. It was escalating very nicely and she wanted to rush off because of her girlfriend. Excuse me? I kissed Sandy's neck and whispered, "She can't wait a little longer?"

Sandy cooed in my ear, "No, she's got an exam and I have to take her."

I cocked my head back and gave her a puppy-dog look and said, "What about me?"

And Sandy said, "How about we get together later tonight?"

I gave her another sheepish look, like well I don't know. I was all worked up and wasn't about to leave without a fight. No, not T.J. "I don't know if I can make that," I said, trying hard to keep her right where I wanted and needed her.

Sandy eased back and said, "Please?"

I'd lost and I decided to give in gracefully. "Okay," I said, "but you'll have to make it up to me in a huge way."

Sandy smiled and said, "Come back around ten and I'll have some champagne and this great hot, chocolate dessert that you'll love. Don't be late because it's ruined if it gets cold."

I stood up and gave her an Opie Taylor look, then said, "I can't believe you're going to put me out."

Sandy stepped right to me and gave me a hug. "I don't want to make Bebe miss her class," she said, "since I was the one who talked her into going to get her college degree anyway."

So I said, "Oh, that's great that you encouraged her."

And Sandy said, "Yeah, because she's really smart but gets kind of lazy sometimes and I know all she needs is a nudge and Bebe is off and running."

"Well, speaking of running," I said, "I'm out of here and will see you tonight at ten."

I opened the door and before I left, I hit the bell on the door and it gave a little chime. I caught the pitch and had the key in my head and Sandy looked all confused and I used that pitch and started playing an invisible piano. I mouthed out loud the bebop notes as they came into my head. Then I leaned back toward Sandy and started to fade the notes. She moved in closer to hear and I faded even more. Sandy got closer still. Finally I was just moving my lips and she had to look up. When Sandy did, I planted a super, soft kiss on her lips—and shut the door.

I had a little time left before I had to go to the center and then later to the club. So I stopped by Players to see Daddy-man. I knew he'd be there. As much money as Daddy spends in the place, he ought to buy it if Outlaw ever decides to sell. He was sitting in the corner for what the club calls its Afternoon Highball Special. All highballs are three dollars for visitors and one dollar for club members. Daddy had a lifetime membership in Players. My old man had two highballs at his elbows talking to some young chick—younger than me—in a dark green dress, professional cut with style. She was pretty; nice body, smooth skin, bright eyes, and a sassy haircut.

I said, "Excuse me for interrupting."

Daddy stared at me all glassy-eyed, then broke out in a grin. "T.J.!"

He hugged me and slapped my back and I could smell liquor in his collar. I said, "Hi"—and he cut me off and turned to the young lady.

Daddy said, "This is my baby brother, T.J."

Smiling, she held out her hand. I shook it softly and tried not to laugh. Baby brother? Okay, evidently he was trying hard to wax this girl's panties, so hey, I played along.

I said to her, "Speed here giving you a hard time?"

And she said, "No, your brother is a lot of fun. I was here to get insurance papers signed by the owner and Speed just wouldn't let me leave without having a drink."

My so-called big brother spoke up. "Sherri here is into computers and I was telling her about my job as a maintenance worker at the computer shop."

What maintenance work? What computer shop? Hell, he called me to hook up his VCR! I wanted to die laughing but I just smiled and said, "Yeah, business is booming."

Daddy was too much sometimes! He smiled back, then his eyes got peaked and worried. I turned around and here was Ann. She had on a nice blue dress but as always it was too tight and her makeup was a little on the heavy side. She'd always been cute and used to have a nice body but age had got that spread going and she kind of let herself go. She and Daddy had been friends since I was a shorty. The only thing about Ann that I don't like is the fact that she has a big mouth; not as in luscious, but as in talks too much. As soon as she reached the table she started, "T.J., where have you been hiding this young lady?"

And Sherri said, "Oh, I just happened to run across these two gentlemen here today. I'm enjoying their company. It's nice to see two brothers hang out."

Ann said, "We all brothers and sisters."

Daddy turned red but he had too much to drink to think fast, so I cut in and said, "Ann, you look good."

But Sherri said too quickly, "Not brothers as in African American—blood brothers."

And Ann looked from Daddy to me and squawked like a chicken. I mean good night, John-Boy Walton, that's how country and loud her laugh was and it was truly on purpose.

Ann said, "You believe that they're brothers? Girl, you better go get some eyeglasses!"

"Shut up, Ann," Daddy said.

Ann said, "They're not brothers—that's his son!"

"Ann," I said, grabbing her arm. And she was doubled over laughing so hard that I couldn't move her without yanking, so I just kind of dropped my eyes.

Daddy said, "Baby, this old lady is drunk."

"Drunk," Ann snorted, "I just got here, Speed. Maybe those old trains you used to ride on have knocked some of your brains loose."

Sherri was smirking now and I just hated that Daddy was getting embarrassed, but Sherri figured she'd rub it in a little more and she said, "What about the computer business?"

"It's fine," Daddy said.

Ann said, "He only got one of those handheld computer games that you play football on—that's it!"

Sherri couldn't hold it any longer, so she just started laughing; and her eyes started watering and now Ann was laughing too. Speed was standing there with his lips clenched and his fist choking his highball.

Sherri said, "You all will excuse me."

And I said, "Wait, I'll walk you to the door." Sherri gave that look and told me not to bother.

Daddy downed his highball and yelled, "Woman, if you don't keep those big liver lips outta my business!"

"Liver lips?" Ann yelled. "You old gizzard!"

Speed was waving his arms. "You talk too damn much. If Lee Iacocca could put your lips under the hood of a car, he'd run Toyota out of business."

I knew they would start capping on each other and it could get downright indecent.

"You wanna play the dozens?" Ann asked. "Huh, nigger?"

"Yeah, liver lips," Speed said, hopping out his seat, squaring his feet, and pulling up his pants.

"Hold it!" I yelled. "I'm not having that while I'm here, so both of you just cool out before you get all geared up." I knew I could referee here because Dad knew how I was about fights in public and Ann did too.

Ann walked over by Dad and twisted her hips, looked back at me, then to Dad, and said, "Saved ya!"

Daddy slurred, "Saved your ass, you mean!"

Ann went and stood at the bar. I walked over to get a drink and stopped next to her on purpose. I said, "Both of y'all need to quit it."

Ann just looked at me, and she said softly, "You know I had to get him, baby. Your daddy is always trying to pretend that the clock is running for everyone else and Father Time is pimp-walking for him. You know Speed and I have been friends for a long time but he tries to pretend that he's Mr. Everything and any

48

she say

woman is a damn fool. Speed don't need to be courtin' the young girls no way. He need to sit his old ass down somewhere."

I said, "Daddy-man can take care of himself."

Ann grabbed her drink and said, "Your daddy almost got his head knocked in with a bottle the other night messing around fishing for that young stuff. Ask him." Then she headed for her chair in the Witches Brew.

A pang of fear hit me. Daddy was too old to be fighting. And a young guy too? Why didn't he tell me? The doctor told him to cool it because of his bad ticker! Didn't he know that Shaft shit was played out? Why didn't he tell me? He's supposed to tell me stuff like that! He could have gotten seriously hurt! I walked back over to his table and said, "Daddy-man, what is the matter with you?"

speed

"Aww, forget it, son," I said. "Ann and me are always having it out but she got way outta line tonight."

"Not that," T.J. said. "You know what I mean."

Hell, I didn't know what he was talking about and I took another sip of my drink and said, "What?"

And T.J. started talking fast and hard about a bottle and my almost getting my brains knocked out and my bad heart. Aww, that bullshit? That's what it was. Just like a spade is a spade; an ace is an ace; the moon is the moon; bullshit is bullshit. T.J. got all indignant, not loud but indignant in a bad tone. You know what I'm saying? It was like he was talkin' to some snot-nose punk or something.

I told him, "Boy, if you don't sit down I'm gonna knock you down. Questioning me? Huh?"

T.J. sat down and said, "Daddy, I—"

"I nothing," I said. "I'm the pistol here and you the pee shooter; I'm the big dick and you the wee-wee; I'm the daddy and you the son. Boy, I had you and you ain't have me, so don't ever question me like that or think I gotta report to you like I'm-I'm some child who missed his curfew or something."

I hadn't had to chastise T.J. like that in years, not since that time I found his wallet on the table and wasn't no condom in it.

I remember way back then, asking him, "Didn't I tell you to keep your shit with you at all times?"

I told him that (A) there were too many diseases out there and his nuts would fall off. Then I told him that (B) somebody might

50

try to trap him with a kid that he didn't need and I didn't want to support because anybody that came down my family line was going to get well taken care of so don't start nothing that I would have to finish. How old was T.J. back then? Hell, that was back when he was sixteen and I had to get him straight. Here he was twenty-five, and I was getting him straight on another tip.

I could tell that T.J. was anxious to change the subject because I know from the time that he was a kid that he never could stand me to bawl him out or get mad at him. Look like that would hurt worse than any whupping I could ever give him. I saw him picking at the little napkin and looking up at the ceiling all nervous.

It put me in mind of when T.J. was a kid. When he was oh, around seven, he'd stand at the door waiting for me like that, picking at the screen latch, kicking at some imaginary nothin' with his feet and looking up at the trees 'cause he knew he'd been bad and was gonna get it. I'd always rush home after a long run to L.A. or somewhere. When I'd been gone real long and if I'd made a lot of overtime and a pocket full of tips, I'd forget whatever it was he'd done.

T.J.? That boy would just start giggling and singing damn near: "Daddy-man, when I get to be a famous musician I'm gonna buy you the biggest and best train there is. It's gonna be red, with a big silver whistle that shoots fireworks, and you'll have a big hat and a magic cane and a seat in front. There'll be a bunch of clowns working the cars to make sure everybody laughs. And, and, and we'll have cream soda pop and hot dogs and barbecue and Cracker Jacks with two prizes in it and nobody but our friends and family can ride. And Daddy, there'll be a car just for us and can't nobody ride in there but me and you and maybe, if you want, Reverend Jackson." You know Jesse was the man back then, don't you?

I smiled at T.J. and leaned into him, to let him know that

everythang was cool. And it was. I asked him, "How was that lunch with the radio lady?"

T.J. gave a little mischievous smile and said, "Cool in the end but, Daddy-man, it started out shaky."

T.J. said he told her to meet him at Arturo's and that rich girl he used to mess with came in and clowned. T.J. told me about the big old scene she made and I told him that was too much sugar for a dime and we laughed. My great-grandma used to say that all the time. In Bama, when something crazy happened she'd say, "That's too much sugar for a dime!"

T.J. can think fast on his feet, that boy came up with a smooth story when the girl Sandy came in. He was a stone player, I told him! T.J. said they went back to her apartment, says she got a nice place overlooking the lake. She was obviously making the bucks. I asked, "How was the coonie?"

He shrugged and said, "I know it's gonna be good, I'll get it tonight."

"What?" I said.

T.J. said, "Well, she had to take her girlfriend somewhere."

This girl gave him the blue balls and sent him away with a rock in his pants and no satisfaction? "Aww, T.J." I teased, "Man she playing fetch with you."

He shook his head. "Nah-uh, Daddy, not with me."

T.J. ran his hand over his head and gave me a little 'tude. See, he was so used to getting what he wanted, when he wanted, that he couldn't see it. But I knew this girl had some game 'cause she ain't give it up right then. She was playing fetch.

T.J. said, "No."

"Hell, boy," I laughed, "she's got the bone. She lets you see it, smell it, lick it, but she don't give it to you right away 'cause she want you to chase it. Shoot, after a while that make the bone taste better and she'll have you bouncing around like a puppy dog." Can't nobody fool old Speed. I told him, "Don't go over there."

T.J. said, "What?"

"Don't go over there tonight," I repeated.

She made him wait, didn't she? She rushed off, didn't she? Let her wait and see that he was in demand too. What the hell could she say?

sandy

I've got scented candles, a lace tablecloth, dessert, romantic music, and an empty chair. No man. I broke my neck after what turned out to be a stressful, crappy evening. I had to deal with Bebe's attitude until I dropped her off at school. But I made it without a fight and cross my heart and hope for menopause that was a big plus for me because I certainly was glad to get her out of my car! Didn't she make a big deal out of nothing? Bebe always had to give you drama! I dropped her off and headed for the station so I could find out what in the world happened to my spots! None of them ran. The Lexus dealer paged me three times! Think he was mad? Doggone right he had to be and I was steaming.

I headed for the radio station. I was speeding down Lake Shore Drive trying to get to work so that maybe I could plug in the Lexus spots for *Morning Drive* the next day. Then I could play it off and say something like, "Oh no, the spots weren't supposed to run in *Afternoon Drive*—I said *Morning Drive!*" It could work if there were some duplicates on the log that I could bump. I was blazing smoke down the expressway because traffic was light. All of a sudden, guess what? No, don't guess, I'm irritated enough already. All of a sudden, I saw flashing lights! I checked the mirror and there was a cop car pulling me over.

The officer got out and came to the window and said, "You were going thirty miles over the speed limit."

Lies! I was about ten over. But I knew better than to argue with a cop. He wrote me a hundred-dollar ticket. Now, you know that hurt me to the core! So I crept the last few miles to work because I didn't really want to throw away any more money.

I got to the building and I went right to production. I asked the manager what happened. I must have said it very coldly because he started defending himself and I know he was right. Hadn't I heard the spots? Yes, I had listened to them twice!

Next, I went to check the logs and the spots were slated for the *Afternoon Drive*. Not a problem there. Then the production assistant walked in with the carts—we played them—and guess what? They'd been erased. Blank! People were so careless! Someone must have put the tapes on the bulk eraser by mistake! Those kind of mistakes will make a business go under. But what could I say? I kept my control because that was the professional thing to do. But, boy oh boy, how I wanted to go off the deep end. But what would that solve? I just gave the production staff a very curt speech about taking care of business and being careful. Everyone just looked at me and I turned and walked back to my desk. I called the Lexus dealer and he gave me major grief. He told me that he'd listened for the spots and had other suburban dealers listening too.

I took a deep breath and said, "I believe there is some confusion here that I would like to clear up. The log is usually full in *Afternoon Drive* but I must have spoken in error because I meant to say that I could get you in *Morning Drive* right away *tomorrow*."

"Really?" he said.

"Yes," I said, and kept going strong, adding, "Yes, your spots will run in tomorrow's *Morning Drive* and I'd love to call your colleagues to explain the misunderstanding and invite them to tune in to listen to the spots at that time."

He said, "That won't be necessary."

"It wouldn't be a burden or inconvenience in any way," I said.

I sensed something was wrong. Why wasn't he buying my story? Then he dropped the bomb on me.

He said, "I won't be advertising on your station, Ms. Atkins, because I'm a businessman's businessman—I can only deal with people who take care of business deals accurately and promptly and you have not shown me that, best of luck in the future."

Click!

I looked up and Tia was standing there. She said, "Was that the Lexus guy?"

I was stunned. All I could manage was, "Ah-huh."

Tia shook her head and said, "He called here a number of times and I took the last call."

"What'd you say?" I asked, and I must of sounded pissed off because her eyes got big.

Tia said, "He was mad that his ads hadn't run and you weren't returning his page. I went and checked the log and told him they were supposed to air but there must of been a mistake and I apologized and told him you weren't feeling well and would get back to him as soon as possible."

Oh no! No wonder! Tia had tried to cover for me and I didn't know it, so I had been caught in a bald-faced lie! I didn't even try to hold it in, I just let out a pitiful moan.

Tia said, "I tried to cover for you."

And she had. What could I say? I would have done the same thing. "I just blew it!" I said to Tia. "I'm not mad at you, it's just one of those crazy things and I appreciate you being a team player and trying to help me out."

That was it! So I dragged myself away from the desk, went back to traffic and production, and told them to forget about the *Morning Drive* spots.

Now, after all that, T.J. stands me up? He doesn't call. It's eleven already and I spent fifty-two dollars and seventy-eight cents for champagne, candles, the dessert fixings, and I'm just plumb out of luck. Wonder if they sell that at the store? Luck with men for sale! Where would you put it? In the household-necessities aisle? How about gadgets and notions? Or create an adult-toy section? No, it would have to go right in the cosmetics section. They'd have to put it in a sexy hourglass bottle like the expensive perfumes. You'd be able to spray it all over your body and it would only attract the nicest men. Men with manners, ideals, intelligence, jobs, looks, and sex appeal. You think women buy those low-fat cookies like crazy? Lingerie? There'd be a run on the market. That stuff would make a fortune for somebody and there's no doubt in my mind that I'd be the one who made it to the store and they'd be out. I'd be left standing there looking pitiful like old Mother Hubbard staring at stone-bare shelves. I've had terrible luck with men, believe it. My last fling, and I use the term loosely, as in I should have flung the man out the window, was Dominique.

Do I want to talk about Dominique? Can I talk about Mr. Nique? I don't want to sound bitter, but I am. He was average-looking but had a sex appeal about him that could set candles to melting. It was unreal because most women that came around him felt it. Even Be!

Bebe said, and I quote, "I'd drink that Negro's bathwater."

I said, "Girl, get out of here with that old phrase!"

Nique was a stockbroker for Salomon Brothers and he worked the floor of the Chicago Board of Trade. Now, we've all seen the movies and Wall Street at the closing bell and people are yelling and screaming and pushing and shoving. But it's really like that. I went to watch a few times. The pressure was tremendous! Some days Nique would come over to my apartment giddy, I mean giggly and sweaty, with a dozen dyed-purple roses, a bottle of champagne, half a dozen joints, and he would love me until the sunlight ran orange and the moonlight rose golden. He was really tall. His high school nickname was Tower; and he was lanky all over, if you catch my drift.

Nique loved to lie back in my bed, stripped to bare bones, his

long arms curled around the curves of the headboard, his head
cocked to the side with a sexy grin and his penis giving me a
salute. I liked to crawl toward him peeling away clothes the closer
I got. My breasts would be so tight they'd hurt and my nipples
would be little pebbles that had washed ashore and become em-
bedded in the sandy softness of my skin. I would be so ready for
this man because Nique had a power, a juice, a magnetism that
made the bedroom air breathe in like smoke. He'd be laid back
waiting and I would slowly put my mouth on places sex books
said *to do* and my mother told me *not to do*. And he would just
make a melody out of my name and just sing and sing and sing.
And that kind of praise, that kind of cheering, makes loving
much richer and more fulfilling. I would think that my world,
that my universe, was truly the only current running through my
body at that instant and that the rest of life was a mirage of
events to keep my mind and body busy until I could again land
there. Right there with Nique. Those were the days when the
market was good. The *profitable* days.

But the bad days? The bone is buried market days? Hell. Nique
would show up at the door and start banging before I could even
reach it. Then he'd fuss that I hadn't answered the door fast
enough and why? Didn't I want to let him in? Didn't I know he
needed me? And why wasn't I faster? I must be diggin' on somebody else. Who was the motherfucker? Naw, baby, there's somebody, huh? Then why aren't you more caring? It went on and on
like that sometimes. Then Nique would fall out on the bed, ball
up in a knot, and make a melody out of the amount of money
he'd lost that day on the floor. I would try to convince him to
forget about it. But you can't make people forget things that they
don't want to, can you? Nique's frustration and determination
couldn't help him make money or make love. Many times his
body would remain at ease and he'd blame me.

Nique said, "Why can't you get me in the mood?"

Hell, I wanted to say, "Give me a reason," but what was the point? What good would it do?

Day after day the market got worse. It was a slump and Nique got laid off and he started to trip. The reefer turned into cocaine and the champagne turned into tawdry wine and his lovemaking turned into release for him and a gift from me.

And when I say gift, I really should clarify that. I've searched myself many times thinking about what went on and what was said and a gift is really what it was. A gift on two levels because at first it was like . . . Christmas or an occasion in that you go to the store and hunt for just the right something special for that person, get it wrapped pretty-pretty, and wait with anticipation to find out how it's received. And joy is what you feel if it's received with the love that you gave it with. That's how it started but as he kept taking with no joy, no surprise, no excitement, and no gratitude, then it turned into, well, charity. Charity like when you walk down the street and a stranger asks you for something and you give them whatever change is in your hand or pocket. And if you stop three feet away and don't turn around, could you say what the person looked like? What they had actually said? The way that they had said it? What their eyes looked like? No, because they're not essential to you. You don't even know how much you gave them. You just know it wasn't much to you but enough to appease them. And I started handing out spare love to Nique. Isn't that sad? That's what I realized but he started getting so low that I felt that if I abandoned him what would he have? Then things started coming up missing. Money. Jewelry. Clock radio.

Nique said, "Baby, all I ever take from you is love."

Nique said, "I haven't seen it."

Nique said, "Why are you bugging me about some shit I know nothing about?"

Nique said, "So what, I borrowed the stuff, you weren't even using it."

Finally he admitted it. He'd already stolen the good thing we had going, so I had to let him go.

Why is letting go of something so hard? Why? You don't want it anymore but you're used to having it there even though it's not the greatest but it's there. I guess it's holding down a space that you need filled and sometimes people think that a place holder is better than a bare spot. But uh, I don't know. I guess it varies from person to person.

Anyway, after I broke up with Nique he kept calling, calling, and calling. Then one night . . . God, this is making me tired talking about this . . . one night me and Bebe were coming back to my old place and Nique was sitting on the steps. He had his head down but I knew Nique was high because he was flicking at his pants cuff with his middle finger and humming. That was his high-as-a-space-shuttle routine. Nique looked up at me and Bebe and cried. He just cried. There was snot running down his nose and he reached his hand out to me. Bebe grabbed both my arms from behind—she was walking behind me, see—and she grabbed my arms at the elbows and whispered in my ear, "If you can't truly save him, don't go down with the ship." Bebe is something, huh? She's always right on in times of trouble. "Don't go down with the ship," Bebe said.

Well, I think I'll wrap up my dessert, blow out my candles, and make a midnight run.

t.j.

Why are piano keys white and black? I used to ask that question all the time when I was a kid. Why not, say, yellow and red? I used to ask my mother, who just shrugged and gave me a kiss. I asked Daddy and he gave me some convoluted answer that I can't even remember. It's about, oh, one o'clock in the morning and I've got a torch lamp sunk down low as it can go, putting a spotlight on the keys. The rest of the room is dark like I need it and that question just popped into my head again. But I've finally come up with my own answer. I think they are black and white because those are the contrasts of the universe. The opposites. The polar ends. The conflict of color. The conflict of people who are various shades of black and white. And everybody is stuck on earth together in their right place like God wanted and they can't do a thing about it just like these keys, and although they look alike . . . they each have a special sound like the unique insides of people and that makes things harmonious when they're played together and makes things distorted when they're not. That's kinda deep, I think. And real hokey too, I think. But it feels right, so there must be some gospel to it.

I'm here at home just tapping my feet against the pedals making my baby grand moan and groan. It's painful sometimes when I can't grab my music and make it what I want it to be. I hear sounds. And sometimes the sounds are so far off, like now, and I can't reach the sounds and turn them into my music. I get so frustrated and angry and pissed off when I know that I should be creating and I'm not.

Like now, why can't I let it out? I have this talent and it's like there's this big, nasty, slimy something or other just sitting its fat ass right in the middle of my creativity. A forklift couldn't budge this thing and I know that it's got to go and I want it to go but it won't move and I can't seem to move it. I want so badly to write wonderful songs because it just feels so good when I do and I get all excited and want to jump up and down and rant and cheer and rave and punch the air like M.J. did when he hit that play-off basket. I need that.

I want to be so good at this and to use this talent that God gave me but sometimes, like now, I wonder why did he give it to me? I-I feel like I'm not worthy, like he made a mistake, like I'm wasting it because I can't get the most out of it or I can't get a handle on it, you know? It's hell trying to grab something and you can't catch it. I'm just flapping and kicking trying to do the best that I can and I push myself and then I get all worked up and knotted up inside and I just want to quit. And who likes a quitter? Not a soul catching air. Nobody. And I know I don't. So . . . what? Got an answer? Hell no. I'm tired maybe. Maybe I'm lazy. I don't know what I am except flapping out in the breeze. Why can't I relax? I know. I'll have a sip of champagne.

I don't know how but I'm able to drag myself back in the kitchen. I've got these magnets stuck all over the fridge—unique ones that my friends and family started giving to me. I've got one of Nixon doing the peace sign with the words "Tricky Dick." I've got Donald Duck. Louis Armstrong. A baby grand piano. A snake. A toilet. A Bible. Piano notes. Ruby-red lips. It's so crowded that I had to move my magnetic clip that holds all my bills on it over to the countertop. The thing is about to bust. Overdue. Last notice. But I've got other things to think about. Like those damn boxes. Those boxes sitting in my attic. I'm no-where near them—they're way up in the attic—but I can see them. Those damn boxes. Those boxes and their contents will keep me honest.

I'm sipping this champagne and I'm feeling a little loose now. I drop down and do a few push-ups to get the blood flowing and this old hardwood floor just cries out for mercy. God, I love this old raggedy house. My grandma left it to Daddy and I'm helping Daddy pay the second mortgage. It's a two-story frame house. Hardwood floors. Cracked foundation. Leaky pipes. Drafty windows. Warped stairs. Character! This is an artist's house. No real comfort, just shelter. I don't deserve to be too comfortable—that'll make me lazy, make me kick back instead of kick butt.

I need a song, dear God! I haven't written anything all week and I'm starting to feel funky. I need something to take my mind off it maybe. I should have gone over to Sandy's tonight and hit it. We would have had a lot of fun, I know she would have eased this motor racing around inside of me. But no, I had to listen to Daddy-man. He's always right, though. It's not like I can't hit it later and I need to set the tone, let her know who'll be running things. But she's on my mind.

I'll bet Sandy is pissed off! If I called her right now, she'd probably tell me off but good. No, on second thought, too early for that, she won't want to scare me away. She'll pout. Yep, she'll give me that fake B-girl pout and be mad as hell behind it. Sandy is probably in bed now knocked out. Sleep good, baby, 'cause when I love you I'm going to love you like nobody else has.

Sandy. I can see her pert breasts and taste her skin on the soft part of the inside of my mouth and I can feel my hands slipping up and down the grooves of her hips. Slippery, slippery from our sweat. I can see her strong eyes glaring down at me as she bobs and rocks above me taking time and effort and I'll give it back to her too. I'll give it back to her oh but good. Sweet loving is coming to us and it's going to be sweet-sweet I know because she's sensitive and the sensitive ones go buck-wild under the night-light. Yesssssssssss! And I can't help but smile and try to get up and man if I ain't sprung!

Maybe I'll call Sandy now and shoot on through. Speed is getting old. Let's see, what will I tell her? I'll tell her that I fell asleep. After all the stuff that happened today and in the restaurant, work, and everything that I just fell asleep over at my dad's place and just woke up. It's so simple it's brilliant. Who could argue with that? And she won't want to anyway. I'm going to dial her number right now. It's ringing but no answer. No answer? Huh, where is she?

bebe

The voice on the intercom said, "Come on, Bebe, let me in—don't be mad!" Sandy kept laying on the bell as late as it was.

Finally I hit the intercom and said, "Girl, c'mon up."

I opened the door and Sandy said, "I knew you were here. You mad?" I still was a little but why smoke a bad feeling and let it just waft all over everything?

So I said, "I'm just about over it."

Sandy said, "Good." Then she started to explain about T.J. in the bar and the girl who had fainted and how she got that hickey on her neck and the speeding ticket and the erased tapes and the lost account and her stale dessert and burnt-up candles. Damn! I thought my day was a mess! So I grabbed a knife and a fork for Sandy to eat this dessert she brought over. I wasn't havin' any at this time of night. Chocolate would go straight to my hips and launch a fat attack that my body just wouldn't be able to fight off.

So we sat at my little kitchen table and I told Sandy about Dap and we laughed and started singing old Parliament Funkadelic songs. That music was a little before Sandy's time but she'd been hanging around me so darn much she knew some of the old cuts too. Sandy started doing the Errol Flynn just like I showed her. Then I reached over and turned on the old jam radio station and guess what? I must of been psychic. Do you hear me, I could have been working for Dionne, okay? They were playing "Flashlight" by Parliament, and we started doing the bump. I mean we were jamming. We went all the way down to the floor, hips poppin'. I made a mistake and knocked Sandy into the refrigerator and she hollered, "Watch it!"

And I told her this was serious business and if she couldn't stand the heat get outta my kitchen! And I just kept jamming on by myself. Then I yelled, "C'mon, partner," and grabbed an invisible man.

And Sandy said, "Who are you dancing with?"

I said, "Wesley!"

Sandy laughed, "What's he doin'?"

I said, "He's doin' a split!"

"A split," Sandy yelled.

I said, "Get on up, baby, I don't want you to hurt the jewels," and I just laughed, then turned around and started doing that Spike Lee dance, Da Butt.

Sandy yelled, "Bebe got a big old butt!"

"Oh yeah!" I stuck it out there and worked it on around. Then I jerked up really funny like someone had pinched me and said, "Stop feelin' on me, Wesley!" And then I had to laugh at myself. Now I was pooped and was sweating and I barely made it to the kitchen table to sit down.

Every time me and Sandy looked at each other we'd start crackin' up. Finally she asked how my test went. "Next subject," I said. "Why do they make that shit so hard?"

I just shook my head and Sandy must of read my mind and said, "They want you to suffer in school."

"You mean I gotta pay dues?" I said.

And Sandy just nodded her head yeah and started licking the chocolate off her fork.

"Well," I said, "the teaching assistant has been trying to hit on me." And Sandy promptly reminded me that I said he looked like a bleached frog. And he does, but if he can help me pass, maybe I'll go out with him anyway.

"I don't know, Bebe, don't jump yet—it's just the first test," Sandy said.

I said, "Look, this white boy can't be more than twenty-three—he's working on his Ph.D. in math—ain't that a trip? He's a nerd, funny-looking, and just wants somebody to talk to and I just want to make sure I pass the class and get my diploma!"

"You'll pass," Sandy said.

Sometimes Sandy has more faith than I do, and I went over to the fridge and grabbed out a can of Diet Dr Pepper.

Sandy said, "I can picture your big day!" And Sandy dropped her head back and closed her eyes.

I sat down the same way and said, "Tell it."

Sandy said, "You'll be standing in the back of the auditorium and it will be packed with folks. Me? I'm in the front row dressed to the T."

I said, "Uh-huh!"

"And, Bebe, that little tassel with be flitting around your eyes 'cause you'll be wagging that big head of yours talking to everybody!"

I thought, Sandy's got vision, don't she? But I said, "Tell it."

"And they'll play the march and you'll be taking long, elegant strides with your head held high and be very graceful."

I opened one eye and peeked over at Sandy, and don't you know she was peeking one-eyed back? We laughed. I closed my eye back and sipped my pop and laughed, "Go on."

"And you'll march to your seat and I'll wave, and you better wave back! Then somebody important, somebody, like you say, big-time? That somebody will give the graduation speech and it'll be great—enlightening and uplifting!"

"Yeah," I said. It was turning out to be a good graduation, wasn't it?

Then Sandy said, "The president . . ."

My eyes popped open and I said, "All the way from the White House?"

"No, silly," Sandy said, still sucking on the fork. "The president of the college!"

67

I said, "Oh. Get rid of that fork, you messing up my graduation ceremony."

Sandy winked and flipped it into the sink. She started again, "Then the dean will ask the graduates to stand and start presenting the diplomas, calling name after name, and you'll line up and wait and yell for your classmates and grin and some photographer guy will be down low snapping your picture as you take your diploma and shake hands. Bebe, when they call your name, I'll jump up and holler and do a Patti LaBelle shake and you'll look down at me and frown!"

I leaned over and slapped Sandy a high five. I let my graduation sink in for a few minutes, then I asked her, "Suppose you can't make it for some reason?"

Sandy looked at me dead in the eye and said without blinking, "I wouldn't miss it for the world!"

I had to lean over and hug my girl 'cause that really gave my spirits a boost because my mama and daddy were gone and I had cousins and stuff but we weren't tight like me and Sandy 'cause we were sisters, you know?

Sandy said, "I'll be there."

And I said, "Cool."

sandy

I went to work way too sleepy after staying up so late clowning with Bebe. Mr. Thing did not call and that made my day at the office drag. I went straight home, made some tea, curled up on the couch, and started reading *Upscale* magazine and the bell rings. I didn't buzz anybody in, so I didn't know who it was. I peeped through the keyhole and who was standing there looking damn sexy? This was not a case of better late than never and suddenly I got mad.

I yanked the door open and said, "Lose your way, T.J.?"

And as soon as I said it I realized how I looked. I didn't look good enough to be giving off attitude. I grabbed my terry robe at the throat and touched my hair. I was not looking my best! Dog-gone it, he'd caught me by surprise. No makeup. Hair tousled. And just a robe on and nothing underneath!

T.J. must of sensed it because he said, "You look good."

And I said, "I looked even better last night." I really liked it when I said that.

T.J. smiled and said, "And what a fool I was to fall asleep and miss out on a good thing. But a good thing only gets better with time, so tonight will be more better than yesterday."

This man was smooth, was he not? I had to crack a smile but Bebe's voice popped into my head.

I said, "And maybe never will be the sweetest of all."

Then I started closing the door and prayed that he'd stop me. But he didn't. I stared at the door for a good minute. I didn't hear him move but I knew T.J. was still standing there and I opened the door back up and he stood there looking determined and very serious. His lips were moist and his eyes just gleamed and he unbuttoned his coat and slipped his hands into his pockets and dropped his head against the doorway and I thought, Doggone, this man is too sexy.

I said, "You know you could have called."

He said, "I fell asleep on Dad's couch and you know what kind of day I had and then when I did wake up it was late and I called but you were out with what's-his-name."

What's-his-name? This was an old trick.

"There's no what's-his-name," I said. "You're just trying to throw me off the subject."

T.J. shook his head and said, "I'm telling the truth—you were gone somewhere or were you ignoring me?" Then he said, "A man can't stand to be ignored or left standing holding a conversation in a hallway like a deliveryman with the wrong pizza."

I stepped back and let him in . . . one, because he had a point and two, I know our voices carried and I didn't need to have my neighbors in my business.

T.J. stepped into the living room and took off his coat and swung it on his shoulder. He had a lot of nerve.

I said, "Did I say you could make yourself comfortable?"

T.J. smiled and said, "No, but I never stay where I'm not comfortable."

Now, that's not the answer I was expecting. I was looking for something like, "Can I?" Or "I'm sorry" or "Give me a break" or something along those lines. I just held my hand out toward the couch and he just tossed his coat on the chair and didn't move.

T.J. said softly, "I owe you the loving that I promised you last night."

"You don't know what would have happened last night," I said. "You're awful cocky, too cocky, Mr. Willet."

T.J. said, "Baby-baby, I know the score, don't you?"

What was he talking about? He was trying to throw me for a loop.

T.J. said, "A musician loves by the score."

And he started walking slowly toward me and I started stepping back toward the couch and T.J. kept talking. He said, "Right now you're *mosso,* which in music means agitated."

I stopped walking and said sarcastically, "Really?"

T.J. kept walking and talking. He said, "My *moto* is *lento* . . . My movement is slow . . . but my thoughts are *dolce* . . . sweet . . . and my intentions are *giusto* . . . precise."

By now he had reached me and was unwrapping my robe. I heard it flop on the floor and T.J. held my arms out and brought them in and kissed my hands and said, "*Maestoso* . . . majestic."

He touched my face with the bare tips of his fingers and then dropped to one knee and kissed my belly button. I had to grab the man's head and hold on as he caressed my thighs and gripped my behind and spread butter kisses all over my midsection.

T.J. said, "My desire for you is *fuoco* and *semplice* . . . fiery and simple, unaffected . . . And I will love you *assai appassionato* . . . very passionately . . . and I ask from you only *rubato* . . . which is a give-and-take . . ."

And you can be sure that I did.

eighteen

bebe

I'm on a sex sabbatical. Like that word? One of my professors announced in class that he wouldn't be here next year because he was going on a sabbatical. He didn't explain and I nodded to my other classmates like I knew and they nodded back like they knew.

I met Sandy for lunch the next day and said, "Oh, by the way my professor is going on a sabbatical next year."

I knew she knew. Sandy had a B.A. in business and graduated with a B-plus average.

She looked at me and said, "Oh, it must be nice to take a leave of absence to do career studies."

I said, "Yeah, sure must be nice."

And I picked up the check because my girl had enough respect for my pride not to bust me out for not knowing exactly what it was. Now, I'm no dummy and figured it was some kind of vacation. Why not say that? Vacation. Or independent study? Or leave of absence? College to me seems to make everything difficult. Class selection. Course requirements. Study groups. Exam schedules. Payment. Oh, baby, don't go there. These courses are expensive! And I'd be in deep doo-doo if the bank wasn't paying a third, cheap-butt company ought to pay for it all. But Sandy says something is better than nothing. I say get all that you deserve! I have worked damn hard for the bank for several years and as a loyal employee they should give me top-of-the-line perks just like I give them top-of-the-line output every day.

But anyway, back to my sex sabbatical. I've been on it now for three months and it's been okay. I promised I'd give myself a year away from these crazy Negroes! Let me tell you about the last one. Don't run for the No Doz, the story ain't that long. His name was Duke. With that name I should have known something. His mama was from Texas and loved westerns as a kid, so she named the boy Duke Wayne Roy Rogers Jackson. Now, that's off the deep end, okay? And Duke bought into this cowboy stuff and you can't blame him because his mama was obviously a little strange. But hey, to each her own.

Anyway, Duke never did drop his southern accent and I found it kind of sexy. But sometimes Duke seemed as country as a wooden bowl full of collards. He liked to open two doors at a time and barrel through, swaggering when he walked. When he stopped, Duke would rest his hip back on his hindquarters, which made for a sissy-looking stance 'cause he had one of them high Kunta Kinte butts. But I vouch, will give a legal statement, testify in court, and be cross-examined by Johnnie Cochran that the Duke was not a sissy. Okay? He kept me satisfied.

I'd look at Duke sometimes and we would be at the Laundromat or the produce store and I would be undressing him with my eyes and playing out our love game just as easy as you please. I mean this man's kisses came right off a cast-iron skillet. Even a good-bye kiss was a potential quickie. Duke had a way of nibbling your lip and pulling it gently before he backed away and it seemed to make me want to fall out wherever I was. Now that was dangerous, huh? A lady must have self-control at all times. Otherwise. Well, if you don't, shame on you.

Anyway, Duke would give me that soft, sucking kiss in the bedroom and pull back so easy and I'd think that a string was tied to my legs because they would just pop open. Ping! Legs open! It was embarrassing. It was a low-down dirty shame and I prayed to get over that lust because my mama said too much lust can land you in the hospital or in the nuthouse. Prayer didn't do it. Ego did. Duke had an ego outta this world! I nicknamed him Superdome because of it. I never told him that. That was between me and my girl Sandy. But Duke was so into this cowboy stuff and had the ego to match that he'd walk around in a cowboy hat, boots, and jean shirt. That was okay on the weekend but *all* the time?

Check this out. On my birthday I made reservations for us at the Pump Room inside the Ambassador East hotel. I was clean! Hair laid. Dress laid. The Pump Room? I picked out some bad shoes in honor of the name and the occasion. The shoes had a four-inch spike heel and a strap that came 'cross the front and snapped on the right side with a baby bow. Was I clean or was I clean? If somebody saw me and said I wasn't, they needed to go to confession 'cause they were a lie and the truth wasn't in them.

I got there and Duke was late but I didn't get mad because I knew he worked at the teen health clinic and sometimes the girls came in there in all kinds of trouble. I knew Duke was doing something good and important, so I never really sweated him about being late. Anyway, I was seated and the room was dreamy and elegant and everything was just fabulous. And Duke strutted over to the table with one of the waiters.

Duke huffed and puffed, "He says I'm not dressed properly."

Duke looked like General Custer. I could have slid right under the table. And what made it ten times worse is the fact that we were the only black people there besides a waiter! I was through, do you hear? Through! I told Duke to dress classy, did I have to go to his house and dress him? Huh, did I have to lay out his clothes like a little child? Evidently I did, and I hadn't, so hey, we had to go. But did Duke want to leave? Oh no, Custer wanted to make a last stand. He started getting loud and talking about racism in America. I grabbed his arm and pulled, and cowboy that he was, Duke was still shouting away over his shoulder, firing off letters like bullets. He was gonna call the NAACP, SCLC, the ACLU, and so on.

We went outside and he started yelling at me. I kid you not. He was yelling at *me* because I didn't take his side. How could I? He wasn't dressed right. I'd look as country and crazy as he was if I tried to defend that Hopalong Cassidy outfit. Please!

Duke said, "You said come dressy."

"No," I told him, "I said wear dress clothes!"

We argued all the way to one of his hangouts. Why did he want to go to the High Noon Lounge? And why did I take my crazy butt with him? I was dressed to the T and I was going to his regular cowboy hangout. Already our relationship was strained. Duke only wanted to do that cowboy stuff. I got tired of smelling shit and watching him fall off a horse. Hell, the man never did place in any of them rodeos. The whole point of going to the Pump Room was to treat me to a place where *I* wanted to go, where *I* could enjoy myself.

Duke said, "It was overpriced, racist bullshit!"

I said, "Better bullshit than horseshit!"

Now we were in his club and like I said our relationship was strained. See, we'd been dating for eight months and the only thing that wasn't getting old was the sex. That's the very reason why I said lust is dan-ger-ous. I was hanging around this nut just to get some. Period. I was putting up with his macho bull and his ego-tripping and all that just to get some and that was a crying shame. We went into the High Noon Lounge arguing and he sat down at the table with his boys.

All of them were dressed alike in that cowboy shit and they said, "Duke, where you going all dressed up so fine, man?"

Can you believe it? I wouldn't have believed that there was more than one person on earth (other than Duke's mother) who thought that silly outfit looked good. Duke decided to front me off 'cause he was in his territory with his posse.

Duke said, "She's tired of the horses and rodeo stuff and don't even want to learn how to ride."

I spoke up, "Why would I want to bounce around like crazy on

75

some stallion and be all sore and achy and sweaty when I get through?"

Do you know what Duke said? Get this. Duke said, "You didn't mind last night!"

Uhn-huh! Yes-he-did! He did-talk-under-my-clothes! They all started cracking up. My mouth dropped open and I just stared at him. But when I caught my breath, I said, "That wasn't no stallion, that was a midget pony." And then I held up my pinkie and went, "Whoa, doggie!"

Where was the cowboy humor? Somebody must of died with their boots on 'cause they all stopped laughing and stared at me like they were a lynch mob. I turned to go and Duke grabbed my arm. I jerked away and ripped my best dress. I called him a whole corral of MFs and his buddies too.

I got home quick as I could. I took off my ripped dress, stripped down to my slip, and lay out on the bed. My head purposely fell flush left toward his side of the bed. All I could see was Duke's fleshy pillow and the unraveling lace of my pink slip where Duke had grabbed my shoulder. I could still feel the touch of his fingers and the smell of his Red Label on my skin. I cried! I cried enough tears to put out a 311 fire! But not enough to douse the flames burning in my heart. I was feeling pretty bad and I wanted to feel worse so I let Stevie tell me about "Rocket Love." Then I agreed with the Spinners that love didn't seem to love nobody.

I boo-hooed for maybe an hour when Duke came in . . . I'd given him a key. Miss-take! And he had these pitiful-looking flowers in his hand. He must of raided somebody's yard on the way over to my place 'cause there wasn't a flower shop open. Duke tried to kiss me and I wouldn't let him because I knew. If those big juicy lips started working, I was through and this relationship needed to be Arnold Schwarzeneggered, i.e., Terminated. I have this bad record collection. I've got all the diva girls, Nancy-Patti-Chaka-Gladys-Diana-Jessye-Dionne-Sarah-Vanessa-

Whitney-and-Ella. All the girls. Many times I'll use a record to let a man know how I feel, if it's not working or something. It breaks the ice. Sandy says it's crazy but so what? It breaks the ice for me, so I went over to the record player and put on Gladys.

I said, "Check out this cut."

And Gladys helped me out and told Duke, it was sad but hey we weren't going to make it. By the time the record ended he was at the door, cowboy hat in one hand and the house keys in the other. He moseyed over to the bedroom door and kicked it open with his foot and tossed the keys on the bed.

Then Duke palmed his balls and said, "Let me be the first to say good-bye and you gonna miss me."

And Duke never lied.

But I'm on sabbatical and I'm going to stay on it for a year. Hell, Sandy is getting enough for both of us. She says T.J. is rocking her world, giving her sexual healing, this, that, and the other thing. That first time she said he threw all them music terms at her—all-leg something, coochie-coo that. Anyway, she says T.J. is the maestro between the sheets. I'm glad somebody's getting something good.

How long have they been together now? It's been just about two months and Sandy is a goner. You know how I know? Because Sandy calls and all she wants to talk about is T.J. T.J. did this and T.J. said that. It's cool, though, because she's happy. But there's one thing I'm kinda worried about. They've been mostly hanging at her place, with her cooking and stuff and drinking from her wine rack. The one time they went to his place, Sandy said it was such a mess that she suggested they go out, her treat. She said there were clothes everywhere; old furniture that his grandma had and whatnot.

Sandy said, "T.J. says no comfort makes him more creative."

I said, "The Negro is just nasty is all."

She said, "T.J. thinks it's okay for a guy to be messy and stuff and that the place needs a woman's touch."

Please? That meant for her to go and clean up and I had to stop her.

I said, "Let the Negro clean up after himself!"

So anyway, back to the money thing. The few times that they did go out, Sandy paid. It looks like she's paying and laying too, if you get my meaning. I'm going to say something, but I hate to because . . . well . . . Sandy says I look for negative stuff. I don't. I just look for shit in the game is all. But I'm going to say something. Watch, though, what Sandy says.

sandy

Bebe is always trying to find something negative about a man. She called me up and started in on T.J. and she hasn't even met him yet. What could be wrong with the man already? She doesn't even know him.

Okay, the first time we went out it was my idea on the spur of the moment and T.J. only had ten dollars in his wallet and he told me that. So hey, we went to my favorite Italian place and I paid. The second time, let's see, the restaurant wouldn't take American Express, which is what T.J. had. And the other times we've just kind of cooled out at my place. No big deal. Bebe is worried that he's trying to use me. He is not, it's just that his money is tight. Musicians don't make a lot of money unless they're under contract with a big company. In the little time that I've known him he's been funny, witty, and a gentleman. He's sexy and oh so good in bed. What else could I want?

Tonight T.J. has a surprise for me. He said to dress really sharp. I'm dying to know where we're going. T.J. won't say. I get a kick out of surprises and some people don't but I do. I like the silly putty feeling of anticipation, the nibble of desire you get in the soft part of your stomach while waiting to get whatever it is that's stored up in layaway for you. I've loved surprises since I was a little kid when I got my first big surprise.

Daddy woke me up one morning and the air outside my blanket was cold and it stung my eyes a bit. I stuck the top of my head out from under the covers and peeped at Daddy.

I said, "School?"

And Daddy said, "No, Boo."

He used to call me Boo because it took a long time to get over my fear of ghosts. Every shadow. Every sound. Every faint rush of air. All ghosts. I don't know why I was so scared and I didn't even like Casper because my ten-year-old mind couldn't fathom a friendly ghost. I was logical even then. Anyway, I was snug in bed and I didn't want to get up. Then Daddy smiled and he had the best smile. He worked in construction since high school and made it up to planning supervisor by the time I turned ten years old. He loved wearing a white shirt and a tie to work. That was his dream.

That day Daddy had on his white shirt and blue and white polka-dot tie and he smiled, showing all his teeth. His hair was always cut low, so low that if you ran your hands across the top of his head it felt like a soft sponge. Mama was a social worker and she taught GED classes at church. She loved to make up new words. It was a game for me and her students. Like Mama used to say, Daddy was darksome. Dark and handsome. And he was. Daddy's face was wide and perfectly shaped, no bumps or knots or moles or blemishes. It looked like God had tailored part of the midnight sky around his body. Daddy had big, sharp eyes and every time he winked at me I used to think of that nursery rhyme, "Twinkle, twinkle, little star."

Daddy said, "Get up, Boo, I've got a surprise. Don't miss out!"

Not me! I remember flying out of that bed to get dressed. We got in the car.

Daddy sang to me in jazz, scat fashion, "Sweet secret . . . Sweet secret."

And my eyes got big when we hit the highway. After a long time I remember seeing the sign. It had a little sleet on it but I saw the end of it. Amusement Park. I looked at him and Daddy played like he was so busy watching the road. But I got confused for a minute because the amusement park was closed in the late fall. We had gone that summer with my cousins who were all older and I remember crying boo-hoo tears, as Bebe says, because I couldn't go on the Go Carts. I stretched until my neck popped but I was too short. Daddy drove around a new way, not the way we went that summer, and don't you know there was a guy standing at a rear gate waving us to hurry up. Daddy slipped something in the man's hand and he said something about forty-five minutes. We went in and it was kind of spooky.

I grabbed Daddy's hand because those rides were whistling and moaning in the wind and there were no flashing lights and cheers or kids running around and the place looked spooky.

Daddy reached down and picked me up and said, "My Boo."

We made our way to the Go Carts. Daddy put me down right by that crazy cutout clown with his hand held up too high for me that summer but now I was dead-on.

Daddy yelled, "You're in!"

And out from behind the benches jumped my cousins. They yelled, "Surprise!"

And they ran right past me and jumped into the Go Carts.

Daddy said, "Go on, Boo."

I had tears in my eyes and I just looked up and asked, "Why?"

Daddy said, my daddy said, "Why not?"

My cousins started yelling stuff like, "C'mon, dummy! Nut-nut, hurry up! Do-do-Boo-Boo, c'mon."

And Daddy said, "You'd better go'n."

And it was the best surprise I ever had and to this day I love a surprise. I told T.J. I love surprises, but I haven't told him that story yet. I'll tell him tonight after he gives me my surprise. Where are we going? Maybe it's that new jazz club called the Niche, it's having a grand opening this weekend. Is that it? That's got to be it.

twenty
t.j.

Wrong-wrong, double wrong. Sandy was guessing all kinds of stuff on the phone but she didn't even get close!

Sandy complained that my house was messy, so I dusted it down and even polished the hardwood floors. It looked good. The windows were clean. I kept the place sparsely furnished, first because I didn't want to spend money on tables and chairs. Second because I didn't want to spend money on tables and chairs. I have a baby grand piano in the living room. It's black and shiny. I bought some pillows with black and white stripes and scattered them all around the floor. I've got one old brass floor lamp that Grandma had and I spent two days last year stripping and refinishing it. That's it. I spent ten more dollars for some black and white candles and spladow! T.J. the man was ready. Sandy is going to be so surprised that I cleaned my place up and made it romantic!

I called Sandy and it was five minutes of guessing wrong before I could tell her what I called her for. I asked her to bring a chilled bottle of wine from her rack. That girl has a great stock of wines and we've been sampling pretty good. That's all Sandy has to do is bring the wine. And do you know she gave me attitude?

sandy

T.J. asked me to bring something to my own surprise? That's tacky. I mean if he asked me to bring wine, that means what? I knew I'd be driving because he didn't have a car and that's cool. But if you're going to surprise me, don't ask me to bring anything. It's supposed to be a total surprise. Am I right or am I wrong? I called Bebe and she was no comfort at all.

Bebe said, "Don't ask me—I'm the negative one, remember?"

Now she was being petty. She can be petty sometimes. I was asking for an opinion and she got closemouthed. Isn't that a trip? Any other time Bebe would be talking a mile a minute, putting in her two cents. Now when I asked her something, she wanted to be shy and coy and objective—please!

bebe

Oh, but no. Sandy tore her dirty drawers with me! She had already told me that I make something out of nothing. Now here Sandy was asking me for my two cents? So hey, I kept my pennies for the Salvation Army, folks who would appreciate it. I played crazy and Sandy got mad! I just did it to irk my girl, to have some fun, and it was fun too! I could do that 'cause she wasn't calling about nothing big or anything, so I could mess with her and it was cool.

Sandy put on her snotty hat and said, "Okay, fine. Be that way."

She tickled me with that! Sandy was kind of funny when she got mad and put on those airs. I remember that's one of the first things I noticed about her when we met about four years ago at Women's Health World.

See, I had started putting on weight. Now, I was already big-boned with plenty of meat on me but I was stacked as they say when I was young. Check that, younger. Well, I have to diet all the time to stay that way now. When I want a snack at the bank, I can't grab a candy bar. No, I have to make like Bugs Bunny and eat carrots. Well, the Bugs Bunny in me took a hike one day after I broke up with this guy. I started eating chewy caramel, smooth milk chocolate packed with peanuts, and it all melted in my mouth and right onto my hips! Two weeks later I looked in the mirror and boy did I look terrible! That candy couldn't have done all that, huh? Then I remembered something my great-grandmother said once when I was, oh, eighteen and visiting her in Texas.

Gran was sitting on the front porch, her wig twisted to the side, her heels mashing down on the back of her orthopedic shoes, and her mouth full of snuff.

She said, "As you get older don't always get stuck loving all spread out on the bottom 'cause your body will start running thataway. Be on top sometimes so your body can stretch a little and at least for a little while be lean and mean in the world."

Then Gran spit out a long stream of black juice. I remember thinking, awwww say that, old girl! So Gran must have had a point. So I made note of that and I decided to join a workout class too. I had to do something because my body was teetering on the line between vaboom and kaboom.

So I signed up for a beginners' class. I remember getting there a little early and putting on my tights. I looked in that mirror and I saw a bulge here and a bulge there. Battle of the bulge. I went in my bag and started looking for a bulky sweat top when this sister walked in. She had on these black tights and there were Tootsie Rolls everywhere. There were two on her sides, one up under her chin, and one right there in that rough spot under your breasts just above the stomach. I put my sweats back in the bag. As long as I wasn't the worst-looking one in class, hey, I was cool. We got to talking and she said her name was Carmella and that this was her third time in the beginners' class.

I remember asking her, "Three times?"

Carmella said, "Yeah, I can't seem to make it over the hump."

"Yeah," I said, "it's hard fighting with your weight."

But I told her then and I still believe to this very day that the rules aren't fair. You know, the standards are too strict. You've got some nuts sitting up in an office building in New York or Paris putting clothes on stick figures. Then the magazines turn right around and try to tell the world that's how real, everyday women look. Stick figures! You know how when you were a kid, around four or five, and you drew people, you drew stick lines and put hair and clothes on them. Remember? When you get to third grade, though, you start drawing people how they really look with depth and dimension. Honestly, I do believe those designers and magazine folks flunked third grade. They're sitting up there making tons of money and making the lives of millions of women miserable and they flunked the third grade. Ain't that nothing?

Anyway, me and Carmella went to class together and it was in a back room, way out of the way. The advanced class was in the front, in a window that looked out onto the street. That's why I had picked the place 'cause those girls looked good. They were smooth, lean, tight, and they would be in that window jamming. So we walked past there and peeked in and kept steppin' 'cause we were in the peewee league. Carmella and I made it to the beginners' class and it was full but there was this one person in the corner stretching. She was skinny and she looked real lean and she had on white tights. She was stretching, doing splits and stuff.

I asked Carmella, "Is that the teacher?"

Carmella said, "No."

And the more that girl stretched and did jumping jacks, the more the rest of the heavy folks in the room got mad. I felt it. We, including me, were throwing daggers her way.

Carmella went over and said, "Hi, I'm Carmella."

And the girl said, "I'm Sandy."

And she seemed a little standoffish.

Carmella told her, "You in the wrong class—advanced is in the window."

Sandy said with attitude, "Excuse me?"

I remember thinking, I hope this child don't mess with big mama Carmella because if she does she'd better be a Christian 'cause won't nobody be able to help her but Jesus!

Carmella told Sandy again, "You supposed to be in the window with the advanced folks."

I heard a couple more people grunt, "Yeah."

Sandy said, "I'm in the right place."

And she kept on stretching. Well, that made Carmella mad and I could see that some of the other ladies were mad too. Me? I didn't care that much but I could tell this Sandy was going to have trouble from the group.

Anyway, I remember we started the class and you could hear the grunts and groans and sweat was popping everywhere and folks was calling on the Lord for help, falling all out and whatnot. My arms and legs felt like they were balloons full of water. But Sandy? I remember Sandy was barely breaking a sweat. We all wanted to kill her. That's the way it went for the next few weeks, until the Challenge, and Sandy made an impression on all of us. See, the classes were supposed to rotate into that big front room in the window. Except our class never made it. One day we asked our instructor, this nice lady about fifty who was in great shape, why we didn't make the window.

She said, "The manager says our class is too out of shape to be in the window."

What? Oh no! We all bitched and moaned and felt real bad. Our feelings were hurt. Really!

Then Sandy spoke up. "We all look as good as anybody else. We've worked very hard and I can see all our bodies changing for the better."

Then Sandy started pointing out how Carmella was losing her hips a little. Carmella just smiled! Then Sandy just went around the room and pointed out all the positive changes in everyone. We hadn't even noticed but Sandy had.

Then Sandy made note, "My breathing is better—I've got a touch of asthma and can't exercise too strenuously but I feel a difference in my stamina already."

That was why she was in the beginners' class with us, see? Except she should have just said that from jump street, you know. Then we all felt bad but Sandy didn't let us—she smiled and led the workout that day and we all felt like a complete group for the first time.

In the locker area I said, "We should talk to the manager one day."

Don't you know we decided to go right then? We all marched in that man's office, was a tight fit too, with me and Carmella leading the way. We demanded that we be in the window room next week. That man looked about as uncomfortable as a Muslim at a pork roast, okay? Needless to say, the next week we were in the window and feeling good. That evening, I asked Sandy over to my place afterwards for dinner. We started talking and it was like we had known each other for years.

And our friendship keeps growing and growing and that is one of the coolest things about life—the joy of having a good friend. But I still ain't giving her my two cents—not this time.

t.j.

Sandy looked great. She had on a silk lilac dress with lace sleeves that hung just a hair off the wrist. She had her hair pinned up and little strands dangling on the sides just over her ears. She smelled like crushed roses. The girl definitely had class—she could dress and she was trying to hang with me. I had on my black silk shirt, unbuttoned way down, and black slacks, slightly cuffed. The room behind me was dark and you could hardly see in.

I stood in the doorway and braced the sides with both hands and asked her, "Are you ready?"

She gave a nice half-smile and said, "Yes."

I held my hand out for the bottle of wine she was carrying and she handed it to me and her eyes got cold for a minute but I didn't care. Why should I go out and pay twenty dollars for a bottle when she had a whole rack full of good wine? I took it and held out my hand for her to proceed.

Here was the setup. I had the piano lit with black and white candles and also had candles along the pillows on the floor.

I said, "Nice."

And she mumbled, "Yes."

And I said, "Surprised?"

She said, "What?"

And she started looking around like she'd lost something.

I asked her what she was looking for and Sandy said, "The surprise."

"This is it!" I said, pointing around the living room. "I cleaned up and look I've got candles and a love nest for us right here."

Sandy gave me a very pitiful look and said, "Oh."

Oh? Oh is what she said, so I said, "What's wrong?"

She just sucked her teeth and started pouting and then she said, "Nothing."

Women! This was nice and I know she was guessing a bunch of other stuff but this was romantic. I had candles and the black and white motif going on and I had cleaned up the place and she just looked at it like it was nothing? Effort and thought went into this and she didn't appreciate it.

So I just told Sandy flat out, "Hey, why are you tripping? I've made a nice surprise for you and you seem like you don't dig it."

And she said, kind of nasty too, "T.J., you had me get all dressed up for this?"

Wasn't I dressed too? It went with the romantic thing I had working. Up 'til now, I had always used my mack-daddy routine—I'd never cleaned up for the other ladies like I had for Sandy. Still, all the other chicks really liked my place anyway. What was wrong with her? Now I'm mad and I just sat down at the piano and didn't say another word. Sandy stood there looking silly.

sandy

T.J. just sat down and started pouting like a little kid. He just kept banging on that one piano key and I couldn't help that I was disappointed. Could I? It wasn't my fault that he didn't really realize how important surprises were to me. I was used to big, fabulous surprises from my dad and so this just paled in comparison.

So I decided to tell T.J. how I felt about it. I went and sat next to him on the piano and he inched away. I inched closer and he inched away. I scooted and then he scooted. When I knew he was at the edge, I gave him a hip check and he bounced flat on the floor. T.J.'s mouth dropped open and I started cracking up because he looked silly sitting there on the floor. Finally he cracked a smile and grabbed one of the pillows and tucked it under his body.

I slid onto his lap and then I explained to him about my first surprise. I told him the story and he watched intently and I could see in his eyes that he understood and after I finished I gave him a soft kiss on the forehead and he immediately started to unbutton my blouse. And gently I leaned up and whispered in his ear. I was going to help give myself a surprise. I was going to ask him to do something, and if he did, I was going to be surprised as hell and oh so pleased. So I whispered in his ear and waited for T.J.'s response.

twenty-five
t.j.

Talk about surprises! Sandy threw me. I know I was satisfying her sexually. There'd been times when I was spent and she wanted more, so I know I was the man, that I had the stroke, so man, I was surprised by her request. What's a brother to do? She whispered in my ear that she wanted a total body caress with *no* sexual penetration. Immediately I started to lift her dress to go down on her and she grabbed my face between her hands and shook her head no. What was this? So I had to think a minute. She had disarmed me of two of my best weapons. A body caress? I looked at her for a little help but it was obvious that she wasn't going to tell me more; she wanted to see what I was going to do. I sat there wracking my brain. Finally I grabbed her and gave her a passionate kiss. She actually looked a little disappointed.

Sandy said, "T.J., you love fine but, baby, don't you know that sometime a caress is better than all the heat in the world?"

Hell no, I didn't know that. I never had a hug that was better than some good old-fashioned skin slapping.

"No!" I said to her with all my heart. "No, baby, that's something new and I'm willing to learn whatever it is that you want to teach—show me."

And I thought to myself, I want you to show me!

And Sandy stood up and said, "Tomorrow night right here I'll be back to show you."

Then she got up and left. What was going on?

speed

T.J. came into the lounge and I knew something was on his mind—could look at the boy and tell. T.J.'s mine. I know my son. He came over to my table where me and Outlaw Jack was drinking.

T.J. said, "Hi, Daddy, Outlaw."

No hug or high five or nothing. Just a pitiful hey was all.

I said, "What's wrong with you?"

He just shook his head like nothing and I asked him did he want a drink and he said no. And T.J. leaned forward and grabbed a handful of peanuts and grubbed them on down.

T.J. covered his mouth quick. "These peanuts are too damn hot!"

Outlaw laughed and said, "You ready for that drink now, huh?"

T.J. grabbed my beer—I was having a light drinking night—my son grabbed my beer and killed about half of it.

I said playfully, "Don't you know a man'll bust your chops for dogging his suds like that?"

T.J. wiped his mouth and said, "Let me ask you guys something."

Outlaw was like an uncle to T.J., so right off the bat he said, "Shoot."

And you know me.

So T.J. goes right on and says, "What's a body caress—with no boning or going down?"

Right off, Outlaw said, "No Johnson?"

T.J. shook his head no.

Then Outlaw said, "No crocodile kisses?"

T.J. shook his head no.

Outlaw went, "Awww, that's bullshit! What's this, some trick question?"

"No," T.J. said. "Sandy asked for a body caress and took out my best moves and I didn't know what she was talking about. When I didn't know what to do, she just left."

That girl was playing with his mind. I told T.J. that too. Old Speed knows what's up. You can't pull nothing over my eyes but a pair of shades. A body caress with no penetration? What's that, some of that new wave stuff? I've been screwing for years and I ain't never heard of no such thing!

"She trying to mess with your mind," I said.

Outlaw swigged down his beer and said, "Yeah, I ain't never heard of a woman that ain't want the Johnson unless you wasn't laying it on her right."

T.J. got mad then and said, "I know how to make love!"

"Stop making love," I said, "fuck!"

And me and Outlaw griped palms. Outlaw loves the Temps, so then he did one of them Temp spins and moved away from the table right over to the jukebox, see? And he got some way he jiggle it in the back, don't know how, but every time two credits pop up on it. Outlaw hit a record. Bam! The cut called "Stroking" comes on. Me and Outlaw locked eyes and started laughing.

T.J. was steaming and mumbled sarcastically, "Ha-ha funny."

Outlaw slapped him on the back and said, "See, youngblood, this is what you gotta do."

"I know what I'm doing," T.J. said.

Then I said, "I told the boy right."

Outlaw belched behind some beer. "Must not have, he here asking questions."

"Aww," I said, "I'm the one who schooled you!"

"Me," Outlaw said. "You ain't school me."

I had to laugh, then I said, "Remember when we was fourteen you said that little Shirley down the street was gonna give you some and you asked me if I had had any pussy yet?"

"Yeah," Outlaw said. "And you lied and said, 'Plenty'!"

I had to laugh 'cause I did remember the lie and it sho' wasn't plenty but it was once and that was more than Outlaw had had, so I still was the voice of experience.

I kept the lie, though. "I had plenty more than you, man!" That's what I said to Outlaw.

"Not now," Outlaw capped back.

I said, "Yeah, you way ahead but I tend to leave them crossed-eye, toothless chicks alone!"

T.J. was sitting back smiling now. We were getting him out of his rotten mood.

Outlaw said, "I got Shirley behind that big old tree at dusk and you had told me to do it standing up so she wouldn't get pregnant!"

"Bull," I shouted, knowing I was lying.

T.J. laughed. "Yeah, Daddy-man, that sound like you."

I smiled. "Well, she ain't get pregnant, did she?"

Outlaw laughed. "No, because I was in there but I wasn't shootin' nothing . . . I was so surprised when I finally found it 'cause she kept going 'That ain't it, nope, you missing it'!"

Wasn't my man Outlaw something else?

I said, "But when you found black gold and you started pumping like I said, you went to town!"

Outlaw laughed and we slapped five. Old Outlaw sitting there was on his sixth beer and he stood up and started working his hips. "See, T.J., you got to get that back and hip in it, boy, and work it on 'round like this here."

Ann and the ladies sitting over at the Witches Brew started cheering and Ann, Ann she hollered, "Get down, Outlaw—hey now!"

Outlaw took a bow and then yelled for one of the barmaids to give their table a round on the house.

He turned around to T.J. and stuck out his tongue and said, "See?"

Ann came over to the table with her drink and said, "How's baby boy here doing?"

She knew what we were talking about but she was crazy about T.J. and wasn't going to embarrass him. And I mean T.J. *was not* gonna let her embarrass him neither.

T.J. piped up quick, "Fine, Miss Ann."

Then he gave that look, like don't y'all say nothing.

Ann winked at me and she gave T.J. a hug. 'Cause she knew! Then Ann said, "I just wanted a little toast 'cause I'm going out of town for a few weeks."

I asked where and she said something about a health spa that she'd been saving for and she wanted to go and lose weight and just get healthier.

Outlaw said, "You fine just like you are, Ann."

I stared at him like he was crazy. Let her go! I knew Ann when she was superfine with an eight-ounce Coke bottle figure. Now she was two-liter size and wasn't nothing wrong with her losing some of that. Anyway, we toasted Ann and she went on back over with her girlfriends.

Outlaw turned to T.J. and said, "You straight now, young-blood?"

Before he could answer I asked him, "When are you going to see her again?"

T.J. said, "She's coming over tomorrow night and show me what this so-called body caress is."

I said, "Cool player—that's when you do your do—lay it on her, big man, like the old dudes would."

Then me and Outlaw slapped each other five.

twenty-seven

t.j.

I slept in after sitting up drinking with Daddy and Outlaw last night. I woke up after eleven o'clock and I was starving but I knew that I couldn't eat anything. Damn, those old cats can drink. If the two of them got straws, I honestly believe they could drain all the Great Lakes dry.

By the time I drug myself out of bed, got washed, and made it down to the community center for the free piano lessons I give to the kids, I was wiped out. But I had to make it down there. I think it's important to give back to the community, you know? I remember how Daddy saved so I could have piano lessons and go to music school and stuff like that. I know most kids don't have parents who can or will do that, so hey, I've got the talent and can squeeze out the time, so hey, why not help somebody else? That's what African Americans should do for each other. Arabs do it. They come here and they loan each other money and help each other start businesses, all nestled in our community, thank you very much. And white people? Please—they *always* take care of their own! So I made it down to the community center and I had two students, two little girls. As usual they hadn't practiced enough, so I had to go over the songs and the scales with them twice as much as I should have.

Anyway, I was teaching Shelly a spiritual that she wanted to play in Sunday school, "Onward Christian Soldiers." Ray-Ray came and stood in the door and started booing. I told him to find something else to do to keep himself busy. Do you know he gave me the finger? When I was a kid, I never, ever would have had the nerve to disrespect a teacher or any adult like that.

So I just told Shelly, "Ignore him, you're doing fine."

Ray-Ray said, "She's tired and her hands are all clumsy and whatnot."

Of course he claimed that he could do better and I had Shelly move over. Ray-Ray came and sat down at the piano.

Shelly said, "You stink!"

And I have to admit Ray-Ray was truly stinking. I could see that Ray-Ray's neck was dirty, his pants were ripped in the seat, and he didn't have on any socks. Ray-Ray's hair was wild but he had little bald spots here and there. He was not taken care of. But I told Shelly to be quiet and told Ray-Ray to go ahead. Do you know that he sat down at that piano and guess what? He was worse than she was!

I said, "Uh-huh, just what I thought. Big mouth and no backup!"

Ray-Ray got mad and slammed down the cover and damn near cut off my fingers!

I grabbed Ray-Ray by the collar and he said, "Let go of me, motherfucker!"

I drug him kicking and yelling next door into the boy's bathroom, went right to the sink, and there was the nastiest bar of soap you'd ever want to see.

I picked it up and held it right next to that sassy mouth and said, "Call me that again and I'll wash out that nasty mouth and take my belt and get me some butt."

His eyes got big and then he looked like he wanted to cry and I said, "Ray, saying nasty words don't make you bad and they certainly don't make people want to be around you."

I knew Ray-Ray didn't have friends and I knew that his father wasn't around and that his mother was on drugs, so I said, "Being alone and being a terror is hard work, little man, and you ought to channel that energy into something else that'll make you feel good."

And don't you know he started to relax? I loosened my grip and lied, "I think you've got some talent and I'd like to give you lessons but you gotta do something for me."

Ray-Ray rolled his eyes. "What?"

I said, "Bathe and brush your teeth and the lessons are on."

Slowly I took my hand away from his collar and he flew out the door. Well, that was that. Ray-Ray would either try it or stay away from me and either way my mission was accomplished. But deep down I really wanted him to come back because it's hard on black boys. He didn't have a Speed like me. Wasn't that a shame? I really thought about it. It's cool for a man to have fathered a son but it's even better for a son to have a father around. Ray-Ray was lost in America because he had no father, no man to give him something . . . a look, a threat, a hug . . . was all he needed and somewhere there was a man who thought he was hot property but who had a kid like Ray-Ray trying to grow up by himself. It really made me think how lucky I was to have Daddy. And Outlaw is cool too.

Sometimes, though I would never say it to them, sometimes I feel like a little kid around them. Now, that's not to say anything bad about them, you know, but just that sometimes I feel like I'll never reach their level. It's weird because I love being around them and I care about them both deeply. And Daddy-man is tops in my book and all that jazz and I know he loves me and all that jazz. I know that they know that I'm a grown man but sometimes they talk to me like I'm still a kid.

Youngblood. That's what they say sometimes, "He's just a youngblood." Hell, like last night when I asked them about the body caress? Outlaw started telling me how to make love, you know like I'm some novice or something. That kinda bothered me but they did it with such fun and caring that I couldn't really get but so mad. But the point is I'll never be truly grown in their eyes. And is that bad? I'm not sure really. The way I'm talking it sounds like I think it's bad, but it's not really, although there is a downside to it. But most of all I guess it's okay. It's nice to have people to come to, to look out for you.

A lot of times I hear other musicians, just other dudes period, dogging out their fathers. They say they didn't care about them. Didn't hang around. Never helped pay for food or clothes for them or took them to the playground and the park and stuff like that. Just like Ray-Ray's father. And that thing with Shaq was deep, how his natural father showed up to claim him now that he's a millionaire and Shaq kicked the brother to the curb and claimed his stepfather who raised him as his real father. I'm with Shaq on that. The man that's there to bandage that bleeding knee, that's there to show you how to throw hands, that's there to grab your collar for clowning in school, that's there to explain that first wet dream, that's there to give you money for those condoms, that's there to see you graduate . . . all that is a daddy, not just some sperm shooter that got lucky and found a home. I'm lucky to have Daddy-man, and maybe one day I'll tell him that.

Anyway, I left the community center and headed for the club to play my after-work set. The rest of my evening started to drag because I was thinking about Sandy and this body caress thing. I called her on the phone.

Sandy said, "We're still on, okay?"

I said, "Oh yeah, like Daddy says it's on like a chicken bone!"

Did she think I was going to let her out of this one? No way! Sandy told me she'd be over around midnight and that was fine but it took forever for the time in between to pass. And you know, I was seeing what she was talking about—that thing about surprises. I was getting kind of giddy and wondering what Sandy was going to do and what it would be like and how I was going to feel. How should I dress? I decided to go bare bones underneath my silk black robe. When the doorbell rang at midnight, I didn't answer right away. I let her ring three times before I strolled over to the door.

Sandy had on a trench coat and was carrying a big black brief-case.

"Job interview?" I joked.

"No," she said, "but I *am* here to go to work."

And I tell you Sandy didn't crack a smile when she said it either. What was she up to? Sandy walked right past me and I heard something go clang. Clang? What is that, I thought, but Sandy kept on moving and went upstairs to the bedroom.

When she got to the doorway, she stared down at me and said, "Give me fifteen minutes, then follow the instructions that you'll find in the envelope taped to the door."

I gave her my most suave smile and blew her a kiss. Sandy turned into the bedroom and shut the door. I went straight to the kitchen and poured myself a drink. This chick had me going! I mean I didn't know *what* to think. Envelope? Instructions? What was she doing? I had no idea, but damn, I was excited.

The only clock in my kitchen was shaped like an old sun. It was hanging crooked, had a cracked ray, and since I had been too lazy to put batteries in it, it didn't even work. I could have choked myself! This was no time to be without a clock! So I decided to revert to my junior quarterback days and started counting, one thousand one . . . one thousand two . . . one thousand three . . . By the time I got to one hundred and eighty I was gaga! I had to stop and think of something else.

I started thinking about Sandy, her body. I envisioned her breasts and the curve of her waist. I heard the catch of her breath and the way she tries to hold back a grunt and the way it makes it sound even grittier than she'd ever really want to be. What was she doing up there? I started to pace a little and then I went into the living room and sat down at the piano. I hit a few notes, trying to play out this good, excited feeling I had. There was a hell of a song here. I closed my eyes and thought, C'mon, Sandy girl!

Then all of a sudden there was no sound. Nothing. Did I go past the fifteen minutes? I didn't think so but I wasn't sure. So I got nervous and afraid that'd spoiled it. I started running for the stairs and on the way up I slipped and stutter-stepped down three of them. My steps are birch and I heard that old wood go *clunk-clunk-bam!* Imagine it, *clunk-clunk-bam!* Then I looked up at the door and Sandy didn't move. Nothing. How could she miss that loud racket? She didn't even come to the door to see what happened! But the note was there. Slowly I began walking up to it. It was a colored envelope, lilac, an envelope like you mailed greeting cards in. I opened it and on a sheet of paper with a rainbow swirl across the top it read, "Put on the blindfold and knock three times when you're ready and when you enter you are at my mercy and cannot speak or move unless I tell you."

I looked around and there tied around the doorknob was a white silk scarf. I tied it around my eyes and held my breath. I knocked three times and waited. I heard the door open. When you lose one sense, the other senses get keener. That's what people say. And you know what? That's for real. I heard the door squeak and hit the back of the wall and I could tell by the sound of Sandy's steps that she was barefoot.

She grabbed me by the collar of my robe, kinda like how I had grabbed Ray-Ray, you know real firm, but there was no anger, just something else. I can't put my finger on it. Anyway, Sandy pulled me in and led me to the bed. I smelled a bunch of stuff but nothing that I could single out. It's like I was smelling some of everything but nothing in particular. Is that possible? Well, yeah, anything is possible.

Next Sandy peeled off my robe and she sat me down and all

the while she guided me by the fingertips only. I felt like some love-handicapped person because my senses were screaming things at me and I had no control. Sandy was in control.

She pushed me back on the bed and turned me on my stomach. Then I felt this warm, mushy something that smelled like coconut and Sandy was swirling it around my bare back and she was humming. Know what she was humming? She was humming the song that I'd played at the J-108 party where we met! She was humming my song! And her hands swirled, just the tips now, swirled and swirled, and she leaned closer to my ear and I could feel the heat of her breath against the inside of my ear. Sandy sat on my back and I felt her hot fuzziness against the small of my spine and I knew she had no clothes on. And her fingertips were strong yet soft. She was pressing hard but not too hard, yet my back started to hurt. It was as if she'd tapped into muscles that I didn't know I had.

Very soon the ache went away and then there was this energy, this current, that started pulsing through my body. I wanted to yell and I was biting the pillow and I felt it building up in my gut and I wanted to say something and I just clenched my teeth and made this sound. It was like when water, not oil, like when water hits a hot skillet and lasted about as long as it takes for the water to evaporate. It was a light, high, quick sizzle that I let out and I just hung onto the pillow. I was feeling ten fingertips and she was working so that her body was rocking up and down and I could feel the insides of her thighs against the outside of my hips and then. And then. Instead of her fingers I felt the tip of her tongue. The very tip, mind you, and it sampled down the middle of my back, then she stopped. Sandy stopped cold.

And I had to say, couldn't help but say, "Baby, please."

And she turned me over and I was still blindfolded now, and she was lying beside me while I was flat on my back and I felt the bed give when she reached and got something.

Then Sandy said, "First smell, then taste."

She ran something in front of my nose. It smelled like straw-berries. She pressed it against my lips and I ran my tongue along it, strawberry, then I took a bite and let the fresh acidic juice run down my throat.

Sandy ran something else in front of my nose. Banana. I tasted with my tongue, then I took a bite.

The next thing, it had a clean oily smell but I couldn't really put my finger on it. I tasted with my tongue . . . ground peanuts . . . and I started chewing and the hardness rolled around in my mouth and it felt good.

Next I smelled something sweet, and I stuck out my tongue but there was nothing there, then I felt this warm liquid hit the top of my tongue and I yanked it back in and Sandy laughed and I swallowed the stickiness down. Syrup.

Now everything was going and every sense was excited—my body, my mind, my sense of smell, touch, taste—and I could hardly move. I was so excited and wrapped up in all this.

Then she said, "Smell."

And I knew the smell. It was cologne, Giorgio. Then I stuck out my tongue and she covered it with her mouth and gave me a deep, passionate kiss.

She raised me up and slid behind me and whispered in my ear, "Let me hug you."

And she wrapped her arms around my neck and I could feel her breasts against my back and her legs against my thighs. And I am not ashamed to tell you that I felt the warmest, coldest chill run through my body and I actually had a profound sexual sensation and I grabbed her legs and just trembled.

And Sandy said, "So, how do you like the full body caress?"

sandy

T.J. said, "I'm a man's man and I'm not ashamed to say, I never thought that I could feel that good outside of sexual intercourse."

Didn't I show him?

"T.J.," I said, "when two people connect physically like we do, it's not just all straight sex—it's about body chemistry and touch and the senses. I mean it was as good for me as it was for you."

"Really?" he said.

I told T.J. honestly, "You don't think that was *just* pleasing you?"

He mumbled something lame and I just laughed and hugged him tighter. Men think that everything sexual is tied into them. What they want. What they feel. What they need. I was there too. I, like all women, have a sense of self and need for satisfaction too. Do men have to think we're along for the ride *all* the time? We like to drive too!

I said to him, "You know, women have fabulous ideas about how to please and be pleased."

T.J. kissed my hand and rubbed it up against his cheek and said, "I see."

I told him, "You need to be more sensitive. Get in touch with your feminine side."

T.J. said, "If I had a feminine side, I'd be touching it all the time!"

And we laughed. Then a long moment passed and T.J. said, "This is one of the best nights I've ever had."

Then I said to him in a shy way because I was feeling kind of unsure right then, not before, but just right then, so I said, "Can I say how stupid-giddy-wonderful that makes me feel?"

"You just did," he said.

I wanted to cheer for myself. And sitting there together felt good. It was warm, skin on skin, and just us.

T.J.'s eyes began to adjust and he said, "Oh, I thought I smelled flowers."

I used construction paper and staples to make little holders. I put a flower in each and taped the holders all across the headboard.

"What all did you have in that jumbo briefcase?" T.J. asked.

So I showed him. In the briefcase I'd brought my little Presto cheese-sandwich maker, a small stapler, a small wooden bowl, Q-tips, construction paper, three roses, Baggies with strawberries, a banana, syrup, a small bag of peanuts, and a travel-sized container of cocoa butter. I used the Presto to warm up the cocoa butter in the little bowl.

"That, that"—T.J. was stuttering a little bit—"that's what went clang."

I just leaned into the moonlight to make dang sure he saw me and I winked at him. We sat there for a few minutes and it got cozy. And we talked a little, about Ray-Ray—I hope he comes back because it's clear he needs somebody and that somebody could be T.J. Then we talked a little more, about jazz, then not about anything really and it just started feeling better and better.

T.J. started answering me with a batch of faint hmmmm?-uh-hmmmmms.

He was so tired. I eased out of the bed, grabbed one of his robes out of the closet, and headed for the kitchen. As soon as I walked out of the bedroom into the little hallway, I heard this noise, like a creaking sound. A couple of paces to my left was this door that was cracked. I pulled it open and looked up the stairs and saw that the attic door was open. T.J. showed me the house but we didn't go up there. T.J. said it was just some old things of his grandmother's up there and a bunch of dust and moths. I tipped up the stairs to close the attic door and the floor was frosty. I reached up and touched the knob and I saw all these boxes.

In one corner of the attic alone, there were eight boxes stacked up. There was a closet door open and there were boxes in there too. One of the boxes nearest the door was open and I tipped over and looked inside. It was full of cassette tapes. T.J. had cut a record! His face was on the cover of the tape and it was a head shot and his eyes looked big and pretty and he had his hands clasped like he was praying or expecting something awfully good to come to him. The title said, "Sweet Love . . . A Debut by T.J. Willet." He didn't say anything about this. Why? I picked up one of the tapes and blew really hard and shook it, trying to get the dust off. I flipped the tape over and looked at all the songs listed. None seemed to ring a bell and all were written by him. I slid one out of the case and held it toward the moonlight to read the label. Suddenly I was grabbed hard from behind. Grabbed by the upper forearms and that made my muscles pop and my hands sprang open and the tape dropped and cracked against the floor. T.J. pulled me up, turned me around, and asked not angrily but more melancholy, "What are you doing in here?"

I told him about the door creaking and trying to shut it and seeing all the boxes and just looking.

T.J. reached down and closed the flap down over one of the boxes and said, "C'mon."

I turned him around to me and brought his chin up with my hand and asked, "What?"

He wouldn't respond. I wasn't going to let it go.

I said, "Why didn't you say that you had produced a recording?"

"I didn't," was T.J.'s response. "You see where they all are."

I sat down on a box, grabbed both his hands, and pulled him over to me. "Tell me," I said.

He hemmed and hawed and said it was no big deal and he

107

turned away but I could tell that he wanted to talk. He wanted to say. You know how someone looks funny, holds their stomach, breathes heavy, and drops their eyes? They want to say. T.J. wanted to say.

I joked, "Well, we'll just be sleeping up here, then, because I'm not budging and neither are you."

That got a snip of a smile that lasted about a second. Then I said again just loud enough so he could barely hear me, "Tell me."

t.j.

Oh, yeah, right. What was I going to tell Sandy? That my grandmother put a second mortgage on her house and Daddy cleaned
out his bank account all to pay for studio time, backup musicians,
and the producer and manager who were supposed to launch my
career. But all they did was cut a few tapes and stall around.

Eventually they said, "Hey, give us some more cash and we'll
take the music to the radio stations and get it played."

But they split and never came back. Was I supposed to tell her
how I broke down and begged my then snotty rich-bitch girlfriend for five grand to keep them from throwing Grandma out of
her house? The house I live in now. The house that Grandma
and Grandpa raised my father in, that I played my first song in
and Grandma said, "Let your little light shine," and the only
place that she ever wanted to live and die?

Was I supposed to tell her about failure? When it happened, I
looked up the word in the dictionary. I wanted something concrete to go with my feelings. The dictionary said fall short.
Become bankrupt. Weaken. Not succeed. It was as if Webster
was defining what had happened to me to the T. Sandy was asking me to tell her about how that failure haunts me and my
work.

Could I tell her that? Everything inside me yelled no! Why
not? And I said to myself, Naw, dude, naw. Because Sandy wants
a man, a strong man and a dude just can't go around looking
weak to a woman. Especially not a black woman. Black men are
always made to look like we can't hang, can't cut it. The world

tries to say the black woman is carrying our race and the brothers are hitchhiking.

I'd already shared with her about Mom and that was enough. Anyone can relate to a sick relative, a sick parent. That's okay. That's universal. But this thing with my first cut? With the music? That was all me. What I couldn't do. What did Sandy know about failure? Nothing. She'd gone to college and graduated. She was the top salesperson at the radio station. Her boss, Harvey, dug her and had promised her good things. She had a nice apartment and a new car. Sandy was a success. She wouldn't have even been able to relate to what I was talking about. She dug me because I was good-looking, talented, and a champ in bed. Yeah, she wanted to be with me and I didn't need to share something that could make her second-guess me. The Twelve Disciples armed with Bibles and crowbars couldn't have made me tell that. So there she was sitting on a crate of my tapes, her legs crossed and a sexy little knee peeking out from my robe, which was way too big and hanging off her shoulder.

I said, "Let me tell you this."

And I leaned in, kissed her under the neck, grabbed her up off the crate, and spun her off her feet. She liked that and I was glad. Sandy just laughed and I stopped her laughter with a sweet-sweet soft kiss.

She hugged me and said, "You still didn't tell me."

I stood there hugging her waist to me and I said, "It was my first try and it didn't work out. My manager wasn't about jack. That's why I'm managing myself and saving for another attempt. I'm saving as much money as I can and I'm writing some hellified music. It's going to be on and that'll be my big break. Everybody will be saying my name. They'll be raving about my technique. About my sound and interpretations. It's going to be on, girl." Then I added, "If you act right, I just might let you hang with me."

And Sandy smiled. "I know it'll be great. Let me help you."

I said, "How?"

She said, "I can help you save and when you get the new recording together I'll get our program director to play it."

Damn, that was cool of her to help me. Sandy knew that I was going to be big one day. I gave her a kiss and that was my way of letting her know that it was cool, she could help me.

sandy

The first check was for $100 to pay the light bill. I couldn't very well leave T.J. in the dark, could I? The second check was for the piano tuning and to fix a pedal that was stuck. T.J. couldn't very well play out of tune with a stuck pedal, could he? The next check was for $272 to help fill the gap on the $600 mortgage. He couldn't very well play out on the street, could he?

Bebe was there one night when T.J. called. I was going to drop one of the checks off at the club. She asked what was going on and I had no reason to lie and I really hate to lie because I never can remember the details and Bebe, like my daddy, can always tell when I'm telling a lie. I just told Bebe I was helping him out. It was the check for the mortgage and I told her about the others too, like the light bill.

Bebe said, "A flashlight and some Energizer batteries would have been cheaper!"

I mean, really. Sometimes people need help. I would help her, right?

"That's different," she said. "I'll pay you back and I won't take advantage of you."

Be went on to say something about a man should not be asking a woman that's not his wife for money. Now, if someone needed help, I was always taught to help. I could see if T.J. was asking me to buy him clothes or expensive cologne or a car or something. He's a struggling artist and he's trying to get on his feet. That's understandable. And I know I would want someone to help me if I was in a pinch. Suppose it was the other way around?

Bebe said, "Of course you should ask him for the money and he should give it to you."

Why? Get this reason. Because he's a man. That's what Bebe told me.

I said, "Bebe, you're a hypocrite."

And she made these funny Donald Duck lips and said, "Yeah, I'm hip."

I said, "I mean, you—" and that's as far as I got.

"I know what it means," she snapped.

And Bebe was very hurt. I was not trying to say she didn't know what the word meant, I was just trying to drive home my point. Bebe took it as though I was saying that she was stupid or something. She's very smart! One of the smartest people I know. I know that she's self-conscious about not having her degree. But she's going back to get it, right? She's about to graduate this year, right? I tiptoed around that one.

I said, "I was just trying to make a point, Bebe."

Then she shook her head, dangling her big hoop earrings. "Whatever," she said. "I saw that picture you all took at the club and the boy is as fine as you say."

"Yeah, buddy!" I said with a smile.

And Bebe winked at me. Then she said, "Women have been throwing themselves at him his entire life probably."

"Yeah," I agreed. What was she up to?

Then Bebe said all nonchalantly, "Wonder if he's still catching?"

I said, "Bebe, me and T.J. are getting along great and he doesn't need to catch because I'm here. We spend a lot of time together and between him working and stuff, the community center, the time with his dad . . . plus, I'd know if he was stepping out on me."

"Stop by the club one night unannounced," Bebe said.

No! I was not above doing some snooping but so far he hadn't given me any suspicions. Why look for trouble when I didn't sense any? I didn't tell Bebe that, though. It made me sound too much like her and the last thing Bebe needed was motivation. I said, "I don't have to do that."

Bebe said, "You're right—I'm the nosy one. I'll do it."

"Don't!" I told her.

"C'mon," she said.

"Cool out," I told her as firmly as I could.

Then Bebe shrugged, "I'm just saying, girlfriend, that you're getting in kind of deep and I've been out here much longer and just don't want to see anything go wrong for you, kiddo."

Bebe sounded like she was a hundred years old or something. I know she's older and more experienced and all that but sometimes she acts like she wants to be my mama, and my mother is happily retired in Arizona. I'm not looking for a mother figure.

"Thanks for the advice," I said as coldly as I could.

And Bebe shot right back, "Is that a nice way of telling me to shut up?"

"Not shut up," I said, "but know when to quit."

Bebe raised her eyebrows, indicating that she really liked that answer. I liked it too. Then Bebe moved in front of the full-length mirror on the back of my hall closet door and said, "Just FYI'ing you, girl, is all—you happy, I'm happy."

I walked over next to her and said, "I'm happy."

Our eyes met in the mirror and I circled my arms around her neck and Bebe said, "Fine, fine as blackberry wine . . ." I joined in. "Fresh off a California grapevine."

Bebe smiled at me and said, "Don't just say it, always *believe* it."

I kind of shrugged at her, "I look fine."

"See?" Bebe said. "You said 'I look fine' instead of 'I am fine.' "

That ego stuff is Bebe, not me. I told her, "Bebe, I'm confident. That ego stuff is you."

"It's not ego," she claimed. "Girl, it's attitude, and I'm just saying believe it because it's true and make sure Mr. T.J. knows it, too."

And I told her that she needed to meet T.J. and see us together and see how good it is and she'd think differently. I wanted Bebe to meet T.J. but she'd been dodging him.

I said, "Bebe, I've been trying to set up something so you can meet T.J. and stop hearing about him secondhand."

"Oh well, I've been real busy with work and class and stuff," she said.

Why didn't she want to meet him? I just stared Bebe down and when I stare her down I can move her like hypnosis. I can move her and she can't stand it when I do it either and Be said, "Don't start."

I kept my eyeballs on her, following her around the room, and Bebe started walking around looking back at me.

"I hate when you do that," she said.

Now I was having fun, so I started humming, real deep, like a chant. I started following Bebe and she just laughed and started walking in circles just to see if I'd track her.

"You so crazy!" she yelled over her shoulder. "If I jump in the lake, you gonna jump too?"

I kept humming and started doing that old beach blanket bingo dance on TV, the swim? Yeah, the swim. But I kept following Bebe, then I threw my hands up like claws as if I would cast a spell on her.

"Evilene from *The Wiz!*" Bebe laughed, and kept moving. Then she said, "Naw, you too skinny for that—more in line with Diana Ross!"

Bebe headed for the bathroom. She was having fun. We were having fun. I followed her right up to the door.

Bebe said, "Uh-un!"

I jammed the door open with my foot and hummed louder.

"Okay," she said, giving in. Bebe agreed to have dinner at my house with T.J., me, and his father, who I hadn't met yet either. I let her go to the bathroom and when she shut the door I stuck my tongue out because I'd gotten the best of old Bebe this time. Hallelujah! When she came out, Bebe got ready to go and said to call when I had a date and time and stuff so she could get her hair together. That was cool. Then we hugged and she left.

But Bebe left something behind. She hit a nerve and I didn't want to address it with anyone, not even with her. Was I self-conscious about how I look? Deep down inside I think everyone is unhappy about some part of their body. I moved over to the mirror. I had to be honest with myself. I felt less secure without her image there next to mine. Why? Why did I need Bebe to tell me that I looked good? Why would I need anyone to approve of what God gave me? But I know that it's more complicated than that. Everyone doesn't like something about the way they look. I know what I don't like and what I am content with. I also know what others may not be pleased with.

So I just stared at myself in that mirror and checked myself out. I liked my hair. My grandma used to say, and Bebe says it sometimes too, it's "good hair." It's naturally curly but I've got a mild perm and that really makes it easy to manage and it's shoulder-length but I've got it cut a bit shorter in the back. I really like my hair.

I remember once, when I was about nine, Mrs. Ellington said something funny to me. She was a black lady who was extraordinarily fair but she had to be black because she lived in the neighborhood; plus she bragged about being a supervisor at Spangle's Department Store because she was the first black they hired. Mrs. Ellington said at first folks, white folks, would come in and try to find her but they couldn't tell her from anybody else. That story was always the second thing out of Mrs. Ellington's mouth, right after hello.

This day, the third thing Mrs. Ellington said to me was, and I quote, "It's a good thing that you've got that hair because if you were nappy-headed and black, that'd be a double curse."

Wasn't that ugly to say that to a child? I remember she was fingering my hair when she said it because back then it was extremely curly. I remember not knowing how to feel. I wasn't sure, because she was smiling and looked pleased, but I was sure that what she said was not a nice thing. I know for sure now of course.

Thinking about that incident made me turn my hands around and examine my skin color. I'm dark. In a box of assorted candy I'm mint-filled. The mint-filled ones are always the darkest candies in the box. And you know what? People pick them last. I've seen it. And I know how that sounds but I can't help but feel that it mirrors our prejudice in life. People go for the white and caramel-colored candy first. That sounds paranoid, I know, but that reasoning, that's what is in my mind and the best way I can describe it.

I remember little boys teasing me about being skinny and black. They called me names like Blackie. Like Spot. Like Tar Baby. Like Licorice Stick. And what was weird was they didn't have any depth to what they were saying because some of them were as dark as me. Sometimes I would cry about it. Sometimes I would pray to God to lighten me up. Sometimes I would throw a penny in the fountain and wish hard for some light skin. One day, me and Mama went to the mall after she got off work—she was a social worker for the city—and we went to one of the malls and it had a big fountain. I threw my penny in the water, stood there, crossed my fingers and toes, and wished my heart out.

Mama said, "Cutie-pie, you'll get that bike you want because your grades are so good."

I told her, "I know. I didn't waste a wish on that."

So naturally she asked what I wished for and when I told her, Mama stopped cold and sat down on the edge of the fountain.

When she scraped together her thoughts, Mama said, "You are beautiful and smart and don't ever forget it."

And I knew I was smart but not beautiful. I remember thinking how mamas are. Everybody is beautiful to their mother—even Renee, who was cockeyed and bucktooth and her mother had the nerve to nickname her Pretty.

Anyway, Mama let that beauty-and-smarts comment soak in for a while, then she asked me what made me wish that. I told her what Mrs. Ellington said, and Mama said, "Wait 'til I see that high-yeller dog."

Then she looked at me, and Mama was a pretty brown, and she said, "Color doesn't matter."

Then I asked her why did she call Mrs. Ellington high yeller, then? I said, "Mama, you're mad and you want to hurt her and the most hurtful and nasty thing that came out first is color. So color must matter if we think of it first and it can hurt so much."

I was a deep little kid if you got me to thinking. And I'd calmed down and started thinking.

Then Mama reached in the water and fished out a penny and put it in my hand. She said, "God made you and we love you like you are."

In the movies that's the miracle scene that makes everything right forever but real life is funkier than that. That made everything all right *that day*. Later that week, some kids teased me and I teased them back about their hair, their weight, or their lack of smarts. And I realized that that's what kids do and no one really wants to hurt the other person. But when we grow up, it stays with us. It doesn't loom over us every minute and my childhood was happy but those incidents, the teasing, those disapprovals, sometimes come back to visit you.

Hair and color are monster burdens for black women. I know for a fact that Bebe can't stand her hair and how proud she is of her light skin. Now, Bebe is not proud in a gloating or negative way against being dark. I never, ever felt that. But she feels very pleased about her skin color and real displeased about her hair. That's why she's always fighting with her hair. Bebe is afraid to get it permed because her mother told her that that would make her bald-headed and she always says, "Better some wild hair than no hair at all." Bebe also said, "Black men don't dig no bald-headed women."

Me? My body filled out some with age and in an era where slim is in, I supposedly got it going on. I'd still like some more chest, hips, and a bit more butt. Not as much butt as Bebe. That's too much butt and she loves it. Her clothes accent her butt and those powerful hips and big breasts. Sometimes I don't like walking into a club with her because I know all the guys are going to eye Bebe. I mean the way they look at her sometimes is so lewd and Bebe can wear some tight stuff! It's not sluttish, but on Bebe with her body and all it makes the imagination start cranking. Bebe says she likes it because working at the bank she has to dress so conservatively and when she's cooling it she wants to bust out. And Bebe, my homette Bebe, doesn't know how to walk. She sashays. Bebe says that's her way of saying, "I'm here and ain't you glad?"

I'm very proud when Bebe handles the guys because at first, most think she's some loosey-goosey-hot-mama-jamma. But Bebe lets them flit around and poke out their chests and survey her land from point A to point B. Then she lets them know that she's for substance. I remember one time we went out and Bebe put on her "Pepsi un-huh" dress and her "sex me" shoes. As soon as we sat down at the bar, a man rushed her and whispered something dirty in her ear.

Bebe quickly told him, "Your eyes are bigger than your wee-wee, baby."

I almost choked on my drink, I started laughing so hard. Bebe could be tough on a brother but when she's into one, she's very caring. Like Duke? She was crazy in love with Duke but claimed she wasn't. But you could tell she was in love the way Bebe talked to him, low and inside. And Bebe had a way of rubbing his upper arm with the back of her hand for emphasis. Or she'd squeeze his hand when he asked her a question and the answer was yes. Bebe loved Duke. They just didn't fit. Bebe is just not a cowgirl but she did love her some Duke.

T.J. and I, well, it's feeling awful good right about now. We've got this chemistry thing going and it's so good and I like hearing him play. He's so talented but I can sense, though he'd never tell it to me but I see it, I can sense at times he's lacking a bit in confidence. Who was it? Marcus Garvey, I think it was. Yeah, he said, "If you have no confidence in self you are twice defeated in the race of life. With confidence you have won even before you have started."

And confidence is hard to keep because life always flips something at you to make you second-guess yourself. T.J. will tell you he has lots of confidence but what he's got the most of is conceit. There's a difference. Confidence is when you show the badge and put it away; conceit is when you pin the badge to your chest and wear it all the time. But you can't really blame T.J. because he's so damn fine and talented. But I have to say, and I'm pleased with myself, that he and I have been spending a lot of time together. We've had some down-to-the-wire racquetball matches, saw some plays at the ETA Creative Arts Center, and we've made fabulous love. A lot! And I've gone to the club and listened to him play during happy hour.

One night at the club, we stayed and waited to give the manager a ride home. His name is Raymonete. He's a Nigerian from France. Raymonete has an elegant voice and stately manner. People coming to the club love him. T.J. and Raymonete get along famously, always kidding with silly knock-knock jokes. That night, Raymonete was in the back counting bar stock, and the place was otherwise empty except for T.J. and me.

T.J. lifted me up and sat me on top of the piano. I sat there kind of like Lena Horne in one of those old movies on cable. He ate it up as I faked a vamp or two for him. Then T.J. played a beautiful melody that I hadn't heard before. Each note resounded in the bottom of my thighs and inched like an army on a mission with no tolerance for desertion; just one massive body of rank-and-file feeling. It moved up and up and fanned out until I could feel it just about everywhere, even in my pores.

T.J.'s music is like that sometimes, not all the time, but sometimes. Behind that conceit he has immense sensitivity. T.J., I think, likes to hide it. That's likely the worst rein holding men in this world, the perception that sensitivity in a man is weakness. I think that notion has crippled what could be the ideal relationship between men and women. But I've glimpsed the sensitivity of T.J. In his music. And in another way too.

Last week, I was picking him up at the community center where he volunteers. Naturally I went straight to the music room but it was empty. I knew he hadn't left, so I started roaming around looking for him. I heard noise in the pool area and there I saw him. There was T.J. looking too fine in a pair of red Speedos. That boy had body just for you! A bunch of kids were at one end and T.J. was at the other end with a little girl. She was standing on the edge, her legs ashy and trembling, staring down at T.J. He was talking to her, trying to coax her into the water.

"Don't be afraid, I'm here," T.J. said.

He spooned some water onto her toes and she wiggled them with an anxious smile. T.J. touched her with confidence and her steps were timid as T.J. talked her into that water.

He held her around the arms underneath the shoulders and told her, "Relax and just let the water take your body."

T.J. was teaching her to float. Later he had her kick. Then T.J. dunked her playfully to wash away the remaining fear of the water. It was his other side that he seemed to save for the kids, for his music, and at times for me. But I want and need more for me. But I don't want to push him. Time, I think, will bring it to where it needs to be.

speed

I went over to T.J.'s to check my boy out. It was a cold, snowy afternoon. I shook some of the flakes off as I stepped inside the house. I noticed T.J. had some new curtains—white with borders of black and red with little piano keys on them. Lady's touch, I thought, and smiled to myself. T.J. was in the dining room on Mama's old hand-carved birch table putting together a model train I had given him as a gift. That brought back a flood of stories my daddy used to tell me.

Years ago, before I was born, my father's first job was for the railroad. He was down South then and Daddy led the crew that would have to straighten out the rails that had gotten bent out of shape by wear and tear. My daddy said the other dudes used to bring molasses or baloney sandwiches for supper but he loved sweet peaches.

Daddy said he'd spin open that mason jar with a flick of his palm, stare everybody else down, and suck down those peaches. He said the sweat would run off his jaws and juice would drip off his lips onto the tracks. "Lord," he said, "them tracks would sizzle and blow smoke back up at him like a low, black dragon." Daddy said he'd grip his hammer like it was a sword and he was King Arthur with his knights and they'd go after that dragon stretched out before them. He must of felt that he was somebody's somebody then!

When Daddy and Mama moved to Chicago, he got a job in the steel mills because he couldn't get a job as a porter but he still loved those trains. Man, he'd buy me trains to play with and later

I got to collecting them. I've got a great collection at home. T.J. was just a little something when I got him to putting together trains from kits, just like he was doing now.

T.J. said, "You're just in time."

I checked out where he was in the project. There was a small piece, the door of the caboose, and I needed to hold it for him. I said, "All right, player, this is like old times?"

And T.J. said, "You know it, old man."

I held the back of the caboose delicately with my thumb and index finger. T.J. used glue and a pair of tweezers to get the piece into place. We just rapped as we worked. "Man," I said, "I thought you were coming by the lounge Tuesday night—watch the glue, not too much."

"I know," T.J. said.

"You know what? That you forgot to stop by or that you still using too much glue after all these years."

"Both," he answered, and kinda grinned a bit at me.

T.J. said that he was out with Sandy and couldn't get away.

I asked him, "I know this Sandy is a nice girl and all but I don't wanna miss nothing, y'all getting serious?"

T.J. answered very quickly, "I'm not ready to get serious about anybody, Daddy, not now. We like kickin' it together and we have fun is all."

I took a hard look at him, then I moved his hand over and helped him steady the piece.

T.J. said, "What?"

I said quietly, "Don't get too serious now 'cause you just twenty-five and a young dude should play, have fun."

T.J. said, "C'mon, Daddy, I'm my own man."

I was pleased because the boy is too young to be getting serious already. I told him, "Young dudes should sow their oats! That's what young dudes are *suppose* to do." All of a sudden I got a craving for hot chocolate. I said, "Something's missing."

T.J. smiled. "Hot chocolate like Mama used to make for us."

I just nodded yeah.

T.J. asked me, "You still miss her?"

How could I not? I told him, "Mama was something else. T.J., your mother was a rare woman—she was beautiful, caring, sweet, funny, and the type of woman a man wants to settle down with. Shoot, my lady was tops!" Here we were talking about Shine. And I told him, "Yeah, I miss Shine."

Shine is the nickname I gave her because her real name was Agnes and that was too old and crusty and heavy for a woman as lighthearted as she was. We'd met at a church picnic and no, I wasn't no member. I'd stopped going to church when I got old enough to run with my old man, and Mama couldn't do anything about it. I'm not a "sinning on Saturday, shouting on Sunday" dude, but one of my partners was. He'd joined the church to meet women and he told me about this chick he was courtin' named Agnes.

I thought, Hell, I'll go see what the commotion is about, and I honestly thought she couldn't have been much if she was spending time with Mel. My man Mel was a nice guy, but boy was he a homely dude. The ladies in the clubs wouldn't give him no puddin'-tane. Period. So he kept hanging out at the club on Saturday night hoping to get lucky and catch somebody drunk and in a charitable mood. The next day, on Sunday, Mel said he would go to church to search for Miss Right.

So I went to this church picnic and I saw her sitting at a table surrounded by three big bowls of fruit. The bowl right next to her arm was full of red grapes, and the way the sun hit her skin she and them grapes looked damn near the same luscious color. She was the prettiest woman I'd ever seen! She had beautiful wavy hair and I knew she had some Indian in her somewhere. And Mel introduced me and I said hello.

She said, "Any friend of Mel's is a friend of mine."

And that's when I knew Mel had to go. Me and Mel wasn't going to be able to hang anymore because I wanted this woman and I was going to have her. And that's just how it happened too. I had to give it to Mel, he didn't get mad but once, and I didn't have to beat him down but once, before he let it go and left me and Shine alone.

Shine was a good girl, a churchgoing girl but she had vision. She loved me and looked at me with love and accepted me as I was, not like she planned on making me over. She never tried to change me and God bless her I sho' did appreciate that.

T.J. said something and I was thinking about Shine and them grapes and I didn't hear clear and I had to ask him to repeat.

My son said, "I miss her too."

I know he did. He was only a little bugga when she died and that's tough on a kid. I look at him often and think how proud his mother would be at what a good kid T.J. turned out to be. No drugs. Law-abiding. He's smart. He's talented. He's good-looking. And he listens to his daddy.

I told T.J. I say, "Boy, play that song for me."

"What song, Daddy?" he asked.

And I said, "You know."

T.J. knew. I wanted to hear that song he wrote for his mother when she was real sick that last time. She was down-low sick then. Her mind had long ago started to fade, but that T.J. could play that song and Shine would smile, nod her head, and feel better on the inside because I could see it come through on the outside.

T.J. said, "I don't remember it."

Now, I've asked him before to play it and he always says he's forgot it. And damn if I didn't need to hear it right after the funeral but T.J. said he forgot it just like he was saying he forgot it now. I know he hasn't. T.J. ain't the forgetting kind but T.J.'s a man and a man got a right to do as he pleases. I didn't realize T.J.

was looking at me and I just told him, because I wasn't sure I had told him before, but I said, "Son, life deals. All you can do is catch the cards because you ain't never gonna get a chance to cut."

T.J. didn't acknowledge my words, he just asked, "How about that hot chocolate?"

"Player," I said, "I'm ready for it."

We walked into the kitchen and I checked the clip on the fridge door. That's where T.J. kept his bills. I noticed some of his overdue notices were gone. I popped the few he had left with my index finger and said, "Hit the number?"

And T.J. said, "I wish!" and handed me my cup and saucer. "Sandy is helping me out."

"Oh," I said. "Well, I'm liking her more and more 'cause she keeping you outta my pocket. Hell, if she's helping pay your bills, how come you haven't been coming by Players Lounge more and buying the old man some drinks?"

I mean I'd been kicking him down with a bunch of money here and there, and he could at least come in and buy a round.

T.J. said, "I'm saving to make another recording, Dad."

I was not necessarily pleased with that. T.J. had nearly bank-rupted us all the first time and he was in a deep depression after-wards. It scared the shit out of me because of the way his mama went. But he said it with such confidence and authority that I just said, "Good."

Then T.J. went on and told me about how Sandy said she'd get her radio station to play it and all that sounded good. T.J. said they wanted me to come over for dinner with them and one of her friends at Sandy's house. I had seen her briefly, only waved 'cause I was in the car heading to catch a train. I was going out of town to Vegas with a couple of my old railroad buddies. I started telling T.J. about this young schoolteacher around thirty-eight who I hung out with most of the trip. I told T.J., "I rocked her world like y'all young dudes say!"

T.J. said, "Daddy, you know you the man."

Damn right! I told him I would go to dinner, wasn't no problem at all, just let me know where and when and Speed would
slide in like grease. That pleased T.J. and I sipped the rest of my
cocoa, then I hugged him and turned it into a headlock 'til he
agreed to come over to the lounge with me to meet Outlaw.

When we got to the place, Outlaw hadn't got there yet. I ordered us both a beer. The waitress brought over a double shot of
Crown Royal with mine and I told her, "I didn't order that."

A voice behind me said, "I did."

I turned around and there was Ann. Baby, baby! Ann looked
like a whole nuther person. Check that. Ann looked like the old
Ann. Damn, she must have lost twenty-five pounds and her haircut was short and sassy. She had on a sharp red pantsuit with
little gold buttons. Ann looked good! Do you hear me? I got up
and faked a heart attack and said, "Baby, you killin' me, you so
fine!"

Ann playfully grabbed my hands and said, "C'mon back to life,
baby, it's me, and I'm staying fine this time."

T.J. gave her a kiss and said, "You look fabulous."

I gave her a kiss. I gave her a big kiss! Then I gave her a hug
too!

And Ann said, "Whoa."

I said, "No."

Then she laughed and sat down in between me and T.J. Ann
said, "It's good to be home!"

I said, "Where did you go and why don't the rest of America go
too?"

Ann said, "That spa was wonderful. They told us about eating
healthy, cutting down on liquor, exercise, and all that. I'm going
to stop eating meat because it's hard on your system. And Speed,
you should think about it too, with that heart problem you got."

Ann was going overboard now!

I said, "Shoot, I eat everything on the pig but the oink, all the cow but the moo, and leave nothing behind from the chicken but the cluck!"

We all laughed.

Ann said, "And my next step is to stop smoking."

"Right on for you," I said.

T.J. said, "Miss Ann, you got it going on, girl!"

Then he drank down his beer. Ann ordered a Diet Coke and T.J. bought a round and then said he had to split.

I said, "Man, you ain't been here but an hour, sit your behind down."

My son said, "Daddy, I told Sandy to meet me at the Jazz Matador where one of my boys is playing sax tonight. You know I got to back up my partner, right?"

Bullshit! I told him that too, I said, "Bullshit, T.J.! You ain't hung out none with your old man, and you running after this same chick like crazy."

T.J. looked like he was getting mad but he knew to let only so much bass get in his voice. T.J. said, "Why are you trying to pick a fight?"

Ann said, "Speed . . ."

I gave her a look and she turned her head.

I told T.J., "Boy, take your sorry butt on."

He gave Ann a kiss and told her how good she looked again, then left.

Ann lost weight but she didn't lose that fat mouth. She said, "Seem to me like you a little jealous."

Can you believe that? How am I going to be jealous of some girl who's dating my son? How foolish is that? I said, "Ann, don't start no dumb shit, okay, 'cause we getting along mighty fine."

Ann grinned. "I struck gold in that coal mine brain of yours, huh?" And she leaned forward and knocked on my head like it was wood.

I had to laugh. "Stop it and buy me another drink."

Ann signaled over her shoulder and the waitress nodded, "Cool." Ann said, "Don't get mad, Speed."

What? What now? And I said, "I won't, Ann." Then I gave her an angelic look.

Ann said, "Please!"

I took her hand. "Say it, girl—say what's really on your mind."

Ann said, "Be careful how you advise T.J. I think he really likes this girl."

"What's that mean?" I asked.

Ann said, "Anybody that keeps him out of here so much has got to be good for him."

Oh, so now this lounge wasn't good enough for T.J. and it was low-class. That's what she was saying and I told her if it was good enough for me it was good enough for my son. Ann started pleading with me 'cause I was hurt now but I wasn't going to show her.

Ann said, "I don't mean nothing bad, Speed, you know I'm crazy about T.J."

I knew that, yeah, but she wasn't his mama. She wasn't his blood. I knew what was best for my son, not her. I said, "Ann, you don't know what you talking about—I only tell my son what I think and he's a man and a man makes his own way, his own decisions. T.J. is a man."

Ann said, "T.J. is a man who idolizes his father."

So? I was somebody to idolize. I told Ann plain, "I take pride in myself and my appearance and I ain't no crook and I respect people and God." Old Speed told her, "I always held a job and took care of my wife, my son, and my mama and daddy when they got old. I paid a bunch of money for nurses so they wouldn't have to go in a home. I'm a fair man and a good friend. Damn right he should idolize me."

Ann backed down then, yeah, she backed down. She said, "Speed, you making it too harsh, baby, I know you."

Then she took a sip of pop and looked down at the coaster, not at me. "Did you ever tell T.J. our secret?"

No! I wouldn't tell him that. Why? For what? What would be the point? I told Ann, "No and there's no need to and don't you tell him neither."

t.j.

How can a grown man act so much like a spoiled kid? Daddy and I had rapped at the house and had a brew at Players. So what was the deal about me leaving early to hang with Sandy? Daddy should have been trying to talk to Miss Ann. She looked good! He should have been trying to rap to her instead of clocking me. Sandy does not have a hold on me. She does things for me and I like to hang with her, nothing deep.

Anyway, I grabbed a cab and headed to Sandy's job. I had it all planned and had left a message that I would meet her there, we'd take her car over, and after a couple of sets we would hang with the band a bit and then crash at her place. Ideal. I got to her job and the guard rang her line and then said she was coming down. Sandy got off the elevator and she had on a pair of jeans and a sweater. Her attire would not do. You had to look sporty-cool to go to the Matador.

I said, "Baby, what's up? Go change or we'll be late."

Sandy said, "Late for what?"

Duh? I said, "I told you two weeks ago about tonight, plus I called and left a message that I would pick you up here."

She forgot! The look on her face told it.

She said, "I forgot, but I didn't get a message to remind me. Our voice-mail system is screwed up."

I knew that. That's why I had left a message with somebody who promised to put it on her desk. I said, "You didn't get a message on your desk?"

Sandy shook her head no.

Now I was a little pissed but decided to just move on. I said, "Just go get your stuff and we'll zip home and you can change and maybe we won't be too late."

Sandy said, "T.J., I can't—I gotta work late tonight!"

Stop the bus. I told her about this two weeks in advance and now she was trying to leave me hanging? Work! Forget work. I told Sandy to go for a while, then get up and come into work early tomorrow.

Sandy began a chorus of excuses about how important this account was. Oh, but I wasn't important? She'd rather stay cooped up in that office than go on an important date with me? That made about as much sense as Rain Man on *Jeopardy!* Now I was mad but I was trying not to go off.

I said, "Well, give me your keys and I'll go over for a while, then double back and pick you up later tonight."

Sandy said, "Aaahhh . . ."

I held out my hand. Sandy just left it hanging there. Finally she asked me to move over to the corner by the phone for more privacy.

Sandy said, "T.J., you don't have a license."

Duh? Like I didn't know that. It looked like Rain Man was going to make it to the *Jeopardy!* finals. I said, "I know, but that doesn't mean I don't know how to drive."

Now she started hemming and hawing. She said, "But your license is suspended."

What was the big deal? My license was suspended because of outstanding parking tickets—not moving violations. I was careful moving, I just wasn't careful parking. She knew this. I hadn't asked her to drive before and it was cool; but since she was leaving me hanging, the least she could do was save me double cab fare, right? I'd already come way out of the way to pick her up.

Sandy said, "I'll give you cab fare."

I told her, "Who just got a speeding ticket?" Her ass!

She just looked, then said, "T.J., my insurance won't cover you and what if something happens?"

Women! Women worry too much. I wasn't driving to California . . . I was going a total of six miles there and back. I couldn't believe it! I said, "Forget it, Sandy." And I turned and walked away.

Sandy said, "T.J.!"

Forget it! I flipped up my coat collar, turned around, and made it through the wind and slush and hit the corner. I flagged a cab and went straight to the Matador.

I missed half of the first set but got there for the last three numbers, and my boy was on. On! He was milking some beautiful sounds out of that soprano sax. The man had a pair of solid-gold lips, period. I shot the breeze with him in between sets and then went back to my seat near a few other musicians I knew. They all had somebody with them. I was the only Negro there solo! My rep was taking a hit and that put Miss Sandy in trouble with me. I sat there sipping my drink.

Someone behind me said, "Need some company?"

I looked up and there was this body. Body a la booming! This woman was in a tight black dress, low-cut, hands on hips, and my eyes roamed on up and stopped at her face. What was her name? From the J-108 party, Tia! I said, "Hi."

And she said, "Is there room for me?"

I said, "Certainly."

Tia gave me a slice of smile and slid next to me. The Matador must not pay the electric bill because it was darn near pitch-black in the club. There were little silver candles glued inside empty jars of Bertina's salsa. The glossy white flames magnified by the glass put a glow on the pale rose polish on Tia's fingertips.

Tia said, "How's it going?"

"Fabulous," I said.

Tia asked, "Are you playing tonight?"

I told her no. She asked about my music and I told her it was coming along and I was planning a recording session in the not too distant future. Tia was leaning in close to me. Now, I knew she dug me from the J-108 party and our little boot knocking, but I wasn't sure that she hadn't seen me at the radio station in the hallway talking to Sandy. So I said, "Where are you coming from?"

Tia said, "Oh, home." Then she went on about having a week's vacation and no money to go anywhere but glad to be off work. Tia said, "Sometimes that job is like falling off a log and at other times it's like the log falling on you."

We both laughed and I asked her what she was drinking.

Tia said, "T and T."

So I had the waiter bring her a Tanqueray and tonic. I ordered another for me, then sipped down the drink in front of me. On the sly, I checked out Tia's bulging breasts. She must of stretched that dress across a hanger and slipped into it right out of the tub. Tia leaned into me and I knew she did it on purpose because she faked and asked, "What cologne is that?"

I wasn't wearing any. She was. And God, it smelled sultry sweet. I lied and said I had on my regular C.K.

"I knew that," Tia said, flirting more.

I didn't fault her for lying. What was the harm? She was obviously trying to get with me again after that last loving, and people lied, little white lies, in these kind of conversations all the time. It was understood. Expected. Demanded. Both parties know that.

The only thing I couldn't quite understand was how aggressive she was—before, Tia was a bit more subtle. Now Tia was almost teasing me. I asked her how everything was going at the job. Now, Sandy never mentioned Tia when she talked about her girlfriends at work. I remember Tia saying she thought Sandy had sucked up to the boss to get her promotion. Now, after the way she played me tonight, I *knew* she was sucking up to old Harvey but good. That work could have waited! Anyway, Tia said the job was fine.

Then Tia said, "You and Sandy are dating, huh?"

I told her yes and said, "Oh, a little girl talk at work?"

Tia smiled and said, "No, Sandy and I don't really chat much—we're okay—but I just overheard her telling somebody else in the office about you."

I was dying to ask Tia what Sandy said but I didn't want to seem anxious about it, so I gave her the eye and raised a brow. Tia wouldn't come across with the info.

Tia said, kind of startled, "Oh, she won't mind me sitting here with you—I wouldn't want to get you in trouble."

What?

I told Tia, "Please, there are no locks on me—we're just enjoying the sets—no problem."

Why was everybody acting like Sandy had a ball and chain around my neck? Tia went on to say that Sandy was a workaholic, that she spent too much time slaving for the white man instead of having as much fun as she could. Tia said she didn't like working with Sandy because she pushed you too hard, maybe she should take a vacay or something. Tia was saying all this but not in a nasty way. It was like she was saying it to see if I noticed it too and if I might correct her. That's the way it came across. Tia obviously felt that I would not run back and tell what she said.

"You're talking very freely," I said.

"Well, I know you're a man who knows how to keep a secret," she answered, and then winked.

I caught the hint. She was right. Plus, Tia wasn't being evil or anything like that.

And I had to agree a little bit, so I said, "Yeah, Sandy is a working fool sometimes—but we all could stand a little more play without a doubt."

Before our conversation went any longer, I heard my name ringing out on the mike system. I looked up onstage and my partner was waving for me to come up, and the crowd was clapping. I hadn't heard him invite me to play a number. The way the crowd was yelling, I couldn't have declined if I wanted to. Tia slid out and motioned for me to go and she started clapping too. I eased past her and our bodies brushed up against each other. The club was small. I went to the stage and I thanked the audience and told them I would play a little special number I'd just written called "Dew Drops of Joy."

I like to take my time before I start playing. Daddy-man used to tease me with this Ed Norton impression he'd do of me. Everybody has seen those reruns of *The Honeymooners?* Yeah, Norton would take about five hand motions to warm up before he did anything—golf swing, bowl, or play the piano. Daddy-man would do that at the piano when I was a kid, then he'd play "Chopsticks." I got such a kick out of that too. Man! It was cool. I'd developed a variation on that that I thought was good for show. I'd understate the hand movements . . . hold them in between gestures . . . not as wild as Norton but subtle and graceful. It worked too. I always felt my audience getting tight with anticipation. It was like they let me tune them into the concept of preparation and concentration. Like baseball. It's as much fun watching the setup—the touch of the cap, the lick of the fingers, the working of the neck, the practice swing, and all that stuff—as it is the actual delivery of action. That's what I had mastered.

At the Matador I could feel it in the air. Sometimes when you're in control, you can tell when you're about to have a special performance. When you feel the threads of power unraveling inside your body, the people, the hungry people, will grab and hold onto those threads. They pull and wind them around their bodies and lock in the good feeling and you can rule them at that moment. I played and played and concentrated on each note. The lingering sound was what I wanted, what I needed.

When I finished, the club went wild with applause. I looked over at Tia and she was cheering too. I stood and swung back my coat, put my hands in my pockets, and looked up. It was a cool way to receive applause. I found it let me soak in the acceptance. It filled me back up. I walked off the stage, the energy just pushed me forward and I was driven. My fingers were throbbing as I reached my seat again. I sat down next to Tia and people all around were leaning over touching me, pointing, and clapping. Tia? Tia leaned over and stuck her tongue in my ear. It felt slick and hot and tickled.

Tia said, "I want you tonight." She said, "No strings—no ties—just give me tonight."

Tia drove us back to my place and we unleashed our lust. Tia slowly undressed herself and me. The sex was good, I was satisfied twice and I enjoyed myself. Tia's body not only looked good, it felt good. We lay there afterwards and that's when Tia gave me a scare.

Tia asked, "Am I better than her?"

I pretended not to hear.

Tia whispered, "Sandy?"

If I told the truth and said no, she would be upset. Why take that chance? So I told a little white lie. "Yeah, baby, you are."

Tia smiled at me and gave me a kiss on the forehead, then she said, "Good, because I wanted to be."

Oh-oh. Was Tia trying to make this more than it was? We'd said no strings. No attachments. This was a lust thing. I dealt with it right then, I said, "Tia, I hope that you don't take this as being rude or anything but I want to make it clear that tonight is just a little episode that we both wanted and enjoyed but there's really no more to it than that."

Tia leaned up on one elbow and stared at me for a minute before she said, "I was thinking the same thing." Then Tia slipped out of bed and gathered up her clothes and spoke over her shoulder, "Bathroom?"

I mumbled the answer. What she said kind of threw me. I guess I didn't expect her to take it so easily. I don't know why. But instead of being totally relieved, I almost felt a bit insulted. It seemed silly because that's what I wanted. But it felt funny somehow that she took it like that. When Tia came back, she was dressed and looking for her coat. I started getting out of bed to get dressed so I could go outside and warm the car up for her.

Tia said, "That's all right."

No! It was cold and dark out. I wasn't going to let a woman just go out and sit in the dark on the street waiting for a battery to kick in.

I slipped on my pants and said very firmly, "No, it's not safe for a lady to be out like that at night." I told her to give me her keys and I would warm up her car.

It was damn cold out. The sky had a frosty blue tint and the wind was heavy and made the inside of my lungs feel like ice cubes. I sat in her little Geo, blew smoke patterns with my breath, and beat my hands together.

I don't know if it was the cold or what, but my mind was very clear and I started having these thoughts. Like . . . like I thought about how I felt about Sandy. I'd been having sex with Sandy and I just had sex with Tia. What was the difference?

The obvious was easy. Different people felt different, looked different, responded differently. Why was Sandy better to me? Tia had the better body by far! Hands down or hands on! But Sandy seemed to have more feeling when she loved. More emotion. I felt more from her. And maybe I gave more with Sandy because she gave me more. Could I be falling . . . I've never been in love before. I imagine that love lays you out flat with emotion. I imagine you can't think about anybody else or want anybody else. I've liked women, some more than others, of course. But I can't say that I've ever truly fallen in love.

Maybe I'm imagining wrong. Maybe love is sneaky, like a thief climbing through the window or a con artist on the street who palms the pea while playing a shell game. Could this be that or maybe it's just a more intense like for Sandy? Or maybe I might be falling in love with her. I don't know. The more I think about it, the more confusing it is. I'm not sure how I feel. Is that bad? Naw, I guess not really. I guess it's just life.

sandy

I can't believe I forgot the Matador. Yes I can. I had a bunch of things going on at work. I was trying to woo two new clients and update some radio ads I thought would sell better for my oldest client, Barclay Cleaners. That was my first account and it was special to me and I wanted to have some new ads for their twenty-fifth anniversary. I had everybody in the office I could helping me out. How would it look if I wasn't hustling myself? How can you ask others to work harder than you are? You can't. T.J., aww, I'd like to explain that to him but he's always been a musician and Office America is another trip.

Anyway, I knew not to call him that night. I waited until the next day. T.J. answered the phone and sounded really tired and I knew he'd be tired after hanging with his friends but I had to call kind of early, around nine, because I had a meeting with Harvey at ten. I hoped that the conversation would be short and understanding. I was ready to eat crow with some dip and chips because I didn't want any arguments. Sometimes you just don't want strife, bull crap, or whatever the word that fits would be. Peace is a beautiful thing when you can get it. And I wanted it.

Anyway, T.J. answered the phone and I said, "Hi, honey, I'm sorry to wake you, but I just wanted to talk before my day got started."

T.J. said, "Okay, go ahead."

And I told T.J. that I was sorry about missing the jazz set and that I would try to make it up to him. You know what? T.J. was very understanding. He had a totally different attitude than the night before.

He said, "Just forget it. It was one of those things and I was just mad because I was looking forward to being with you. I'm not mad at you—I'm just mad about you."

That made me feel so good. It took a burden off my mind because I didn't want to fight and carry my wounds around all day. I talked a little more, then we set a date for the big dinner. The dinner with me, T.J., his dad, and Bebe.

The next week flew by. We decided on a Wednesday night because T.J. was off, the bank closed early, and that day was open for T.J.'s father. I decided to take the afternoon off so I could cook the meal that we would have at my place. I debated between a few dishes because I wasn't a great cook, but I could do a lot with pasta. I figured pasta and vegetables and fish would be good for everyone. So I decided on shrimp and linguini in marinara sauce, stir-fried cauliflower and carrots, and a three-bean salad. For dessert, Bebe said she was going to bake one of her fabulous lemon cakes. God, that cake is good. It would make you kill someone for a slice! That cake disintegrates as soon as your tongue hits it. Bebe wouldn't even give me the recipe.

I was going to have some herbal iced tea, beer, and wine to drink. T.J. said Crown Royal too if I wanted to go straight to his daddy's heart. Not a problem. I added that to the list.

The day of the dinner I got off work right on time at noon. Dinner was at six. I had done all my shopping the day before except for the shrimp. I wanted it fresh. I had tried cooking this dish before when two friends from Denver came into town and it didn't taste right because I had put the shrimp in the refrigerator for a couple of days. So I headed to this gourmet fish market about half a mile from the job.

I got there and the store was packed. Apparently, everyone had run in on their lunch hour to shop because the store now closed at one on Wednesday. Since when? The guard said since new management. I got to the back and there was a frenzy. People were huffing and puffing and trying to get waited on. I finally ordered my jumbo shrimp and I told the guy to wrap it while I got some season salt over in aisle three. I jetted over and back, got my package, and headed for the checkout lines. Knock off the "s." There was only one line open. Everybody was going nuts now. Two people called in sick, the checkout girl said. She couldn't have been more than eighteen, and she surely had an attitude about being the only person working. So she was taking her sweet little time. Now, I wasn't nervous *yet*. Annoyed? Yep. I hate it when places do that. They take advantage of their customers. They've got a damn good product, so they never have enough people working because they want their bottom line to be blacker and fatter.

I was in line for thirty minutes and I was behind this lady and her little girl. She was so cute, sucking her thumb, playing with the zipper on her jacket. She had pecan-brown hair gathered in a ponytail at the back with a pink ribbon and sky-blue eyes. Her face was flush and her little cheeks were plum red. She smiled at me and I smiled back. Her mother had a cart full of food and she was using a calculator to add it up. Well, the guard at the door was locking and unlocking the door to let people out. Now, as soon as the little girl got to the candy stand, her eyes lit up. She grabbed a bag of M&M's with peanuts and her mother said, "No, Suzy!"

Suzy jerked away. She yelled at the top of her lungs, "I-wann-it-I-wann-it!"

Her face was turning red. Every time her mother reached for her, Suzy jerked away and tried to bite her hand.

Her mother spoke in a silly, monotone voice. "Now, Suzy, is this the way we behave?"

Obviously. Suzy must have thought she was on camera because she was performing. Suzy fell out on the floor and started kicking. Her mother couldn't move the cart up and the checkout girl couldn't ring the rest of her items because the little girl was having a fit on the floor.

Her mother said, "If you don't stop, we'll have time-out."

Time-out? Time-out where? In the shellfish section? In the spices aisle? Where in the store was she going to have time-out? Suzy took that threat and swallowed it like the M&M's she was shoving in her mouth. Now her mother was trying to stand her up and all the people behind me were moaning and groaning.

Finally a gray-haired black man in the rear said, "Spank Suzy's behind and she'll mind!"

Do you know the woman had the nerve to roll her eyes and get an attitude with the old guy.

She yelled back, "I'll handle the situation without advice from you."

What was her problem? She needed to do something because this kid was out of control. I never would have dared show out on my mother like that when I was a kid. My mother prepped me in the car.

Mama would say, "I just bought you new shoes and a toy and that means no candy or anything else today." Mama made sure I was looking at her too. We'd be sitting in the parking lot waiting to get out and she'd be preaching, "Don't show out on me in this store or you'll be in big trouble when you get home and you know I'll get them legs but good, don't you?"

Oh yes, I knew. Suzy didn't know.

Finally after Suzy ate all the candy and smeared the rest on her clothes, she got up very happy and satisfied. Everyone looked at each other and then at Suzy and shook their heads.

I finally got out of the store and drove all the way home, behind schedule thanks to Suzy-Q. I unwrapped my white package and what was inside—catfish steaks. Catfish! I could have died. Catfish steaks and pasta? I don't think so. Now it was two-thirty and I was in a panic because now I had to run out and buy some shrimp. I flew to two grocery stores and neither of them had any fresh shrimp. Finally I decided on the salad shrimp—one store had some that were fresh and I needed to get going, so that was that.

I got back to my place and it was three already! Bebe said she'd be there at three. Did I miss her? Bebe would have waited, so I knew she was on her way. Anyway, I got started and I threw on some music. I was listening to the trumpet sounds of Leroy Jones playing "When My Dreamboat Comes Home." It's got a nice swing to it and I wanted to work timely. My hair was pinned up and I had curlers in. I was in my slip with a robe on top because I didn't want to get anything on my clothes. I was doing pretty good. An hour passed and I was getting less worried about my end but Bebe was dead on my mind! Bebe said she would come and help clean the dining room and set the table for me. I had newspapers and folders all on the dining room table. It wouldn't take but a few minutes to clean up but I didn't need that extra burden. Finally the bell rang and I went to the buzzer and hit it hard. After a few minutes there was a knock at the door.

It wasn't Bebe. It had to be Speed, T.J.'s father, because he was T.J. with age and he looked good. Before this, the brief time I saw him was in the back of a car. Now he was standing right in front of me wearing a tweed overcoat and a Dobbs hat cocked to the side like my daddy used to wear and I could tell that it was old but well taken care of. Speed probably had the original box the hat came in. He was also holding a little red vase with a red and white rose in it.

He removed his hat and stated, "Sandy, girl, you are a lovely sight."

I was still a little stunned and I said, "Spe—Mr. Willet?"

He laughed and said, "Go ahead, baby, all the ladies call me Speed."

I saw where T.J. got his charm from! I finally cleared my head and asked him in.

Speed handed me the flowers and said, "For you."

144

And I took them and smiled and that's when I noticed the sleeve of my robe! I wasn't dressed! I touched my hair! It wasn't combed! No makeup! I must have looked like a ragamuffin. I started to apologize, "I'm sorry, I wasn't expecting you so early."

Speed said, "No problem, you look lovely just as you are."

That made me smile. I took his coat and he had on dark blue slacks with the band at the waist that closes with a hook and a knit shirt, royal blue with a white and black stripe across the chest. It was an old style but it looked fresh on him. I knew now why he thought he was such a player. Speed looked good. And he had an air of arrogance around him.

I watched as he slowly surveyed and approved of my apartment. I wanted him to be pleased. I felt a little fluttering in my stomach. I hadn't expected to feel this nervous. But this man had such a presence. It was odd. I'd never been around a man who threw off that kind of air. It was like he was a man's man and that drew out all the elements you felt being a woman. I think I was nervous because I wanted him to know that I was good enough for his son.

I told him, "I must say T.J. is the spitting image of you and he's a lucky man."

Speed just winked at me and sat on the couch, legs stretched out. He relaxed his arm and threw it across the back of the sofa. He looked at me and I felt like I was being scrutinized and I just wished I could turn back the clock and be dressed already. What was he thinking? What was he feeling? I didn't know. Couldn't know. I said, "Crown Royal?"

And he grinned. "On the rocks."

I got him his drink and excused myself and went into the bedroom to change. I checked the clock. Doggone it! He was more than an hour early and Bebe was more than two hours late. Where was she?

bebe

I wanted to make a good first impression on T.J. and his daddy at Sandy's dinner. I needed to get my wicked hair together and I couldn't wait to get to my hair appointment with Kay.

My car was back in the shop again, so I got Norma from my job to drop me at home. She waited for me while I ran upstairs. I went, grabbed the cake in the plastic dish, and came back down. Kay suggested that after I picked up my outfit from the cleaners next door, I could change in her back office. Great! Then all I had to do was catch the bus that stopped in front of the beauty shop. It would let me off about a block away from Sandy's place. Norma let me out on the corner and left. I walked half a block to the shop and guess what? The lights were out and the whole place was empty. I looked up and there was a big sign: "Closed— IRS." Then I went to the family-owned cleaners next door and asked the kid who works there what happened.

I said, "Mike, what happened next door?"

He said, "Miss Be, the IRS came in and closed them up. They weren't paying taxes."

I asked Mike, "Well, did Kay leave a note for me or did they say where they were going?"

Mike shook his head and laughed. "No, but check Cook County Jail!"

I said, "Mike, don't joke about a black woman and her hair—it ain't funny a' tall."

Now I was trying to think. What was I going to do? I couldn't go to dinner with my head looking all crazy. I picked up my

146

cleaning and Mike's mother came out and I asked her about any other hair salons close by. She recommended a shop, four blocks away, that her sister goes to and told me to ask for a woman named Naoma. She said Naoma was a little wild but that she could do some hair. Cool! I raced off. I knew I was gonna have to give this woman a hell of a tip to let me just walk in, but hey, it would be worth it.

I got to the shop and it was decorated nicely in blues and greens with track lighting and everything. I asked the receptionist for Naoma and she asked was she expecting me and I told her no. She said Naoma was booked. I started telling my story and then I pleaded to at least talk to Naoma. I didn't know she was standing right behind me.

Naoma was tall, about six three, and nothing but bones slipped inside a black cat-suit. She was a tawny brown color and her hair was like something out of *Essence*. It was laid! It was jet black, glossy, and feathered beautifully. Naoma was thirtyish, smoking some kind of ultra-slim cigarette that was hanging out her mouth, causing her left eye to close from the smoke as she used both hands to blow-dry a woman's hair. Naoma said, "Damn, that's fucked up about Kay. Kay was cool with me!"

I asked her, "Look, can you do something for me—work me in and I'll make it worth your while."

Naoma said, "What did you want?"

I said, "Cut and blown dry."

Naoma said, "Looks like you need a perm."

I said, "Kay just deep-conditioned me. I don't like chemicals."

Naoma took a deep drag on her cigarette. "Look, I feel for your situation but, girlfriend, if I work you in, I ain't standing up here blowing them naps out for no three hours. I'll give you a mild perm and we can work you right on through and out. Trust me. Look at my other two customers going out the door now."

I turned to look and their hair was laid. The ladies were smiling and laughing and touching their hair and I looked up at the clock and then at Naoma.

She said, "Whatcha thinking?"

I looked at her and said, "I'm thinking okay."

Naoma told me to have a seat and she'd get me started in five minutes. Five minutes flew by. Twenty minutes later Naoma got on the phone and started to chat with her daughter.

She yelled, "I said no company and no—no Nintendo until you do your math. Do you want me to come home and get after you?"

I thought, Hell no, because I'll never get my hair done!

Naoma said, "Y'all walk your little butts down here now!"

At that point it had been thirty-five minutes and she hadn't even washed my hair. Two other women were sitting next to me at various stages. One had her hair wet and had been sitting there for about fifteen minutes. The other sister had her hair blow-dried and it was flying out like a lampshade on her head. Naoma caught my eye and I gave her a pleading, pitiful look. Naoma got off the phone. I got up and was going to tell her good-bye. Before I took two steps somebody else walked in and it was a teenaged girl. She was big as a house, eating Fiddle Faddle, and she had half a head full of hair—one side was cut way short above her left ear.

Naoma said, "Hey, Shawonda."

I was ready to kill Naoma and wondered how long it would take to go home and get a hat. Then Naoma sent me, Shawonda, and one of her assistants to the back and she told her to give me a wash and condition and to give Shawonda a red rinse and she'd be back to give me the mild perm.

Naoma said, "I'll work straight through with you, Bebe, and have you out in one hour."

I checked my watch. I'd be late but I was sure Sandy didn't really need my help early. I already had the cake, so I dealt with it. Plus I'd already wasted too much time.

I went to the back and her assistant started washing my hair. The water and shampoo felt and smelled good. I finally started to relax. I felt the wet coolness on my scalp and I felt the assistant combing it through. She stopped and told me to just relax and then she walked over to Shawonda and began working on her.

My head was feeling just as cool.

Now big mama Shawonda said, "It's hot in here."

I said, "No, not really."

Shawonda said, "Uh-huh, I'm burning up and my scalp is tingling. Hey!"

I looked and Shawonda was sitting up fanning her head with the Fiddle Faddle box and caramel corn was flying everywhere. A piece dotted my eye!

Naoma came running in. "What's the matter!" All of a sudden she yelled, "No!"

I jerked up and Naoma faked a smile and said, "Sorry, relax."

Then Naoma grabbed the assistant's arm and took her into one of the booths and slammed the door.

Shawonda? She was yelling, "Fire! Fire!" And her eyes were watering and Naoma ran out and started washing the child's hair. Shawonda was cursing up a storm and hot water was flying everywhere. Shawonda was trying to get up and Naoma was slipping and sliding trying to hold her down. Shawonda was shouting, "That bitch," and her legs were flaying. "I'm drowning now!"

I got up and caught a glimpse of myself in the mirror. And there was all this red gook in my hair. I couldn't help it. And if I could I wouldn't have. I threw open that door and grabbed that assistant by the collar and said, "What did you put in my hair?"

Shawonda yelled, "She gave me a perm and you my color!"

Naoma started rinsing me out and she said, "I'm very sorry."

I was so mad I didn't know what to do. I said, "Color it back."

Naoma said, "I can't right away."

I sat up and she shoved me back down. She said, "Your hair will fall out if I throw another color on top of it right away."

How long was I supposed to walk around with red hair? I told her, "I work in a bank!"

She said, "It wasn't in long and I can keep washing and washing it until it's almost out and there's only a trace left—it'll be okay."

Now Shawonda was raging, "I want to kick somebody's ass!"

I was so mad, I said, "Get her! Get her!"

Naoma told her assistant, "You're off for the day."

For the day? I hissed to Naoma, "She ought to be off for life!"

I was steaming! Naoma led me to the private room where people get weaves and now I'm really stunned. I went into the room and there were two little girls sitting at a side table doing fractions and eating. Guess what they were eating? My famous lemon cake. About half of it was gone. If I had a bomb, I would have dropped it on the place.

speed

So this was Sandy. She was short, a bit skinny. Her face was nicely shaped, dark smooth skin and expressive eyes. I tasted my drink and my impressions. My son T.J. was right. There was nothing physically outstanding about her but there was something unique. She had something. Sandy was just a person you'd remember. It wasn't any single thing about her but the package as a whole. The chick was classy. And she was making some dough from the way the apartment was laid out. She had a bunch of those Kunta Kinte heads and stuff. That African art stuff was back in. She was making bank, yep. That's why she could help T.J. with money and stuff.

Sandy went into the bedroom and started to get dressed. I went into the kitchen. I saw we had some spaghetti and some raw-looking vegetables. Damn, I knew I was gonna have a Big Mac attack later. Then I opened the fridge and she had some celery, carrots, and dip. The doctor would love her. I looked on top of the fridge and saw a bag of Ruffles and grabbed those. I went back to the little bar tray she had in the middle of the room and I made myself another drink. Sandy came out. She had on a fitted knit dress with little beads at the neck and on the cuff of the sleeves. The dress was mauve and fit her like a glove. But it didn't look tight or cheap. She'd gotten beaded earrings to match and her shoes were the same color too. She was put-together. I'm a dresser myself and I know how hard it is to match up some colors. I was impressed.

I toasted her with my drink and told her true, "Very nice."

And Sandy said, "Thanks!"

She went in the kitchen and she tried to make small talk. She asked me about football. I told her, "Hoops is my sport."

Sandy said, "Really? My best friend, Bebe, loves basketball! I'm glad we're having this get-together. You guys will have something to talk about."

I said, "Good."

Then Sandy and I started talking about the weather. How cold it was, and this and that, and I kept filling up my glass. Then I went over to the stereo and turned on the old jam radio station. Sandy yelled from the kitchen, "Good choice!"

I listened to the Temps croon "My Girl" and I bopped in the window with the fabulous lake view. And I let the lake lead. The water was beautiful and it moved me and grooved me. I heard the buzzer sound and I turned. Sandy came out of the kitchen and was wiping her hands on this big red apron she had tied way up across her chest bone. I turned back around and finished my dance with the lake. I knew T.J. would be a little early and he would want to be here ahead of me to check everything. My son says I'm a critical cat. That's why I had to sneak in first. I saw a wave move on the lake so I had to dip. Dip and sip. Sip and dip. I turned around and there was a woman with a booming body—she had butt, tits, and hips Good God Almighty.

Sandy stuttered a bit, and said, "Ahh, this is Bebe."

Then she turned to me and said, "This is T.J.'s father, Speed."

We exchanged greetings. Then Bebe said, "You must be a heck of a dancer with moves like those."

Girl had an eye, didn't she? She knew how to showcase that body too. She had on a two-piece dress that was purple and clung to every mountain and molehill. Pow, Bebe had back. Her hair was fixed nice, cut and styled to accent her face, and she just got it done because I smelled all that stuff women get put in their hair. I said, "Bet folks call you Red."

All of a sudden Sandy said, "Excuse us!"

She dragged her friend into the kitchen. I guess they wanted to have one of them girl-to-girl talks or something.

sandy

Not only was she late, Bebe came with some old store-bought cake and a head full of red hair. Where was she going with that hair? I wanted T.J. and his father to think I had class and style and here was my best friend with this crazy red hair. It looked horrible. Why would she do that? The cut and style looked good, but that color?

I whisper-shouted, "What happened to your head!"

Bebe whisper-shouted back, "Give me a break!"

Give her a break? She was the one who was late, who brought a Louisiana crunch cake and a funny-looking head of hair.

Bebe said in a regular voice, "Why are we whispering?"

I said, "Sshh! Obviously I don't want Speed to hear."

Then Bebe gave me a condensed version of the shop and the IRS and the mistake and the kids.

I said, "Fine, but couldn't you put on a hat?"

Bebe whispered, "Get a grip!"

She always made a big deal out of things that happened to her. If something was important to Bebe, it was the most important thing in the world. Yet this was important to me. And now she was taking it lightly. I started getting the serving dishes ready. I told her I could do it now and I stressed the word *now*. Bebe just sucked her teeth and shook her head, then she stopped at the door, turned, and said, "Sandy?"

I looked and Bebe walked back over and nudged me with her hip. "Cool it," she said. "You're the best and I'll be darned if they won't know it." Then Bebe winked.

I was nervous already and there was no sense in staying totally mad and I just flicked my dishrag at her. Then the buzzer rang.

Bebe said playfully, "I'll let lover boy T.J. in."

Now my mission was to get dinner on and them out as fast as possible. I felt that this was going to be a tense night. I wanted everything to go perfectly. But my gut was singing a different tune. T.J. and his dad both were checking me out. I was the one being judged. I was glad T.J. was here because at least that would take a little of the pressure of entertaining off of me.

T.J. waltzed into the kitchen looking good as could be. He had on a mauve silk shirt—we wanted to match—and some black slacks. His accessories—watch, neck chain, and bracelet—were silver. T.J. kissed me and gave me a hug. And he must of felt it because he said, "Nervous, huh?"

t.j.

I could tell Sandy was nervous so I tried to reassure her. I was going to offer to help but she wanted to handle it, so I let her handle it. I headed back to the living room with Daddy and Bebe. Man, Bebe had some buck-wild red hair! It was styled very fly but that color! Man, it was like a cross between a beet and a coconut. Dirty red. She had a nice body and I knew when I walked into the living room that that's what Daddy-man was digging on. And she was digging on him too. They were sitting on the couch and Bebe had her shoes off and one leg tucked up under her, propping up those big hips. She and Daddy were talking about basketball. Daddy told her Jordan is the best to ever play the game. Bebe talked about those incredible moves the way Mike can stride down the court, body graceful and under super-duper control!

Daddy said, "Yeah, everybody wants to be like Mike."

Bebe cut her eyes and said, "Bump that—I wanna be like Juanita."

We all laughed. Fast girl, wasn't she?

Daddy looked at me and said, "Boy, she's funny."

I smiled and sat down in the easy chair next to the couch and grabbed a couple of chips. Daddy dropped his hand on Bebe's knee and kept laughing. Bebe picked his hand up, dropped it back on the couch, and frowned at me. Huh? Daddy-man wasn't trying to throw a move on her that tough. What was wrong with her?

Daddy looked uncomfortable and then he asked me, "Can I get another?"

I yelled to Sandy, "Sandy, Daddy wants another drink."

Sandy came out of the kitchen, smiling, and she fixed Daddy his drink and asked Bebe if she wanted more wine.

Bebe said, "No, it's right there, I'll fix my own."

I caught that. I knew what type Bebe was already. She was selfish and thought that every little gesture was wasted on a man. I knew she'd already told Sandy that she did too much for me. Sandy had told me so. I didn't say anything to Bebe, just a thank-you to Sandy. I touched her hand. I appreciated her efforts and I wanted Bebe to know it.

Sandy said, "T.J., can you help me set the table?"

I got up and stretched a little and went behind her into the dining room area. It was right off the living room but you could see around the corner. Yeah, Bebe was trying to play it off but she was into Daddy. Out of the corner of my eye, I caught Sandy watching. And she didn't like it either.

thirty-eight

sandy

Bebe is a born flirt. She can't help it. And obviously T.J.'s Daddy is too. Bebe's just too comfortable. I can't believe she is laid out on the couch over there with her shoes off. Why does she need to have her shoes off? She's just too comfy. I just need to forget about it, Bebe is Bebe and that's that. She's going to do what she wants to do, God bless her. So T.J. and I got the dining table all set.

I called out, "Ready for dinner?"

As soon as Bebe and Speed stood up, an old song came on the stereo.

Bebe said, "Hey, now!"

Speed said, "Aw, yeah."

Bebe said, "Chaka Khan."

Speed said, "And Rufus."

Speed started dancing and he was popping his fingers and floating his hips.

T.J. said, "Get down, Daddy."

And Speed really started then. Bebe was standing there and she was watching, she cut her eyes at me, as if to say, not bad. Now, Bebe can jam. But I mouthed to her, "Don't." She frowned. I mouthed the word bigger, "Don't!" And she nodded. T.J. moved into the living room and was kind of cheering his daddy on. Speed decided he's really going to demonstrate his moves. On Bebe. He worked his way over and started to break on Bebe. But she was just standing there trying to play him off. She cut her eyes at me.

Speed said, "She can't help you—I'm the dance master."

I just hung my head.

thirty-nine

bebe

This man was trying to break on me! That after he had tried to feel on my knee. I know I'm a flirt but clearly I was just being polite. Speed had had too much to drink and was getting a little too touchy. So I decided to keep the small talk going and not flirt anymore because he just couldn't take it for what it was, innocent little flirting. I had taken my shoes off because my feet were hurting. There's three things that a body can't stand—two I'm positive about firsthand. One is a toothache. Two is your feet hurting. Those I know. Three is probably bamboo sticks up under your fingernails. I don't know nothing about that but your feet hurting? Hey, relief must be had. I wouldn't have cared if the President of the United States was at dinner, okay? So I already had my shoes off, relaxing, and I wanted to enjoy myself after a crazy day. But here was Speed trying to break on me!

Sandy, my girl, was holding reins on me. And Speed was jacking me up and stuff. Now, you know I could only take so much? And his son just thought his father was all that, and a bag of chips. I like a son and father that are tight like they obviously are. But they were arrogant! Whoooo, these two thought they were sharp and they were, but dog, don't be too bold about it. Speed just cut loose on me. I looked over at Sandy, my eyes pleading, Turn me loose, turn me loose. Sandy dropped her head. That meant she knew there was nothing she could do. So I handed Mr. T.J. my drink and said, "Hold this."

I spun out and got up on Speed just like he had just got up on me. I started swinging to the left. Speed went with me. I started working to the right. Speed went with me. I said, "Cool."

He said, "I'm with you, baby."

Oh yeah? Not for long. I spun out and started working it on round and before Speed could get up on me, I two-stepped out of the way and started working it on round again. I spun back. I hesitated, swung left. Speed couldn't catch Bebe. No, not the Bebe. He looked confused. He'd had too much to drink to keep up with me plus I can dance my butt off. I heard the bass kick in and I started popping my hips and started working up and down. Speed mirrored my move and I said, "How low can you go?"

Speed said, "Down to the floor."

So I headed in that direction. Speed got almost there and lost his balance and sat flat on the floor.

I'd won! So I two-stepped around a bit to rub it in. Did a little shake in front of T.J. Sandy had to smile. Deep down she knew she wanted me to win.

Speed got up and bowed and toasted me before he killed the last of his drink. "Go, girl," he said.

I thought about it. Speed? He wasn't such a bad guy—conceited as hell—but a black man without conceit is bound to be nuked by the world. Conceit is a buffer for the black man. Too bad it couldn't be a bulletproof vest.

Sandy said, "Can we eat now?"

speed

I had to toast her. Bebe had a motor and knew how to run it. I wasn't no sore loser. A loss is a loss. But I don't lose often, so there was nothing wrong with being gracious. We all sat down and ate. But you needed a magnifying glass to see the shrimp.

I joked, "The shrimp has shrunk!" We all laughed and then Sandy told us the story about the fish mix-up and the brat in the store. I said, "T.J. never would have pulled that."

"No-no," T.J. said, "I had home training."

I said, "Yes, sir, me and his mama brought him up right."

Bebe asked about Shine. She didn't know she had gone on. I told her that she had died suddenly when T.J. was a boy. Sandy said that she'd seen a picture of Shine on T.J.'s dresser. Knockout, wasn't she? And Sandy agreed she was beautiful. T.J. smiled. You know, he's always been very proud about how good his mother looked. I told them all that Shine was one in a million. I told them about how we used to take T.J. on early morning picnics by the lakefront in the summertime. I told them about teaching T.J. how to swim and T.J. talked about how fearless he was 'cause he knew his mama could swim so good. T.J. said she was very gentle with him in the water. I wasn't even sure T.J. remembered all that. He remembered, huh? Memories can hold onto a body, yes sir.

Anyway, talking about Shine kind of made me sad, so I changed the subject. We talked about O.J., nutty Newt, and then T.J. said he had a surprise. He said in two weeks a friend of his was having brunch with Oscar Peterson, the famous jazz pianist.

T.J. said his friend knew Peterson's nephew and had hooked it up. T.J.'s eyes were getting big with excitement just talking about this man. Oscar Peterson had flair, style, staying power, and he was one of T.J.'s idols. T.J. told Sandy that he was invited to the brunch and he wanted her to come too. Then he leaned over and gave her a long, passionate kiss. I tapped my glass with my fork and catcalled and Bebe joined in on the fun. They both smiled at that. Then I finished up my meal and excused myself. I needed to get back to Players. I was ready to hang and my boys the Windy City Breeze were playing. Sandy started clearing the dishes.

I said, "Thanks for the nice evening—I really enjoyed myself and the company."

"You are always welcome," Sandy said.

And I had enjoyed myself and it looked like that put Sandy at ease and T.J. too. That Bebe? Lord, she nodded like, I know you enjoyed my company. Bet nothing bothered her. She had spunk and I had to admire that. Bebe offered to get my coat and T.J. was helping Sandy take dishes into the kitchen. I walked up behind Bebe and gave her a little pat on the behind and said, "If you ever want a rematch on the dance-a-thon, come down to the Players Lounge on Seventy-ninth, right off the Dan Ryan Expressway."

She handed me my coat and just smiled. T.J. offered to walk me to the elevator and I told him to come on.

t.j.

I asked Daddy did he really have a good time and he answered yeah. Daddy said, "That was all right. There's something unique about Sandy and she's got class."

He did say she needed to learn how to cook some real food instead of all that veggie stuff—Daddy-man said he was going to grab a Big Mac on the way to Players.

He said, "What about that Bebe?"

I said, "Yeah, she's a ball buster. Sandy let it slip one day that Bebe told her she was going too much for me."

Daddy said, "Bebe should mind her own damn business."

And that's what I thought. I said, "But, Player, she was digging on you, huh?"

Daddy said, "Yeah, you know I pull the ladies all the time. I don't know, though, she's got a lot of mouth."

That's what I thought too.

Daddy said, "But did you see that butt?"

I said, "Yeah, man, she got body by Boomin'."

I said, "Daddy, what was up with the dance—you lost on purpose just to be polite. I think you could have turned it up a notch and beat her if you *really* wanted to."

Daddy hit the elevator button, stepped on, gave me the thumbs-up before the doors closed.

forty-two

bebe

T.J. and Speed were out by the elevator. "Homette," I said, "that Speed is a trip."

Sandy nodded yeah and said, "I saw him palm your knee."

I said, "Girl, he patted me on my behind at the closet."

My girl said, "What?"

I told her he was a hound dog from Beverly Hillbilly days, okay?

That made Sandy laugh and she asked, "But what did you think of T.J.?"

And I know how sensitive she is, so I said, "He's all right. Fine as hell." I told Sandy I just hope he ain't as big a dog as his old man.

Sandy ignored that comment and said, "I thought I was gonna die when you all started that dance contest."

We started? We who? He started it. And I finished it. Speed thought he was smoking me. I told Sandy, "He was okay and actually pretty good for a guy his age but he couldn't hang with the B. Not the Bebe."

Then, as playful as I am, I got a devilish idea. I started imitating Speed right there in the kitchen. I poked my chest out. And that's some poking, let me advise you. And I grabbed a glass and took a loud sip and then I got bowlegged and started rocking on round. I put some bass in my voice and said, "Get down, yeah!" Then I started bumping and grinding my hips. Then I faked like I was going to fall out on the floor. I cracked up and Sandy wasn't even laughing and I said, "C'mon, girl, you know that was funny."

Sandy didn't say a word. But T.J. did.

He said, "Daddy was better than that, I think."

Damn, he was standing right behind me! That shut me up. I didn't mean any harm. I was just having a little fun. T.J. just went to the sink and grabbed a glass of water and went out into the living room. Me and Sandy just looked at each other. I heard T.J. put on an old T-Monk tape and I whispered, "Sandy, I'm sorry!"

Sandy whispered back, "I know you were just playing."

I told Sandy, "Don't be mad at me!"

Sandy was real cool, she was like, "I'm not mad and don't worry about it. I know you were playing. I'll explain it to T.J."

But I wanted to explain it myself before I left. I had no intention of being a third wheel. A third wheel makes the bike ride funny. Now, I didn't know—should I leave? Would it look like I was embarrassed and ran out? Should I go talk to him? What? I didn't mean anything, you know? So on the way out I stopped by T.J., who was sitting on the couch. I said, "T.J., people always say I play too much and that's just what I was doing in the kitchen there, clowning. It was just a joke and I didn't mean any harm."

T.J. smiled and said, "No problem. I was a little put out at first—but fun is fun."

That was so cool of him, wasn't it? I felt much better. I went to get my coat and I gave Sandy the okay sign as I passed the kitchen door. That was really cool of him to take it like that.

sandy

As soon as Bebe left, T.J. let me have it. He started talking about how rude that was to make fun of his father. I told him I wasn't making fun of his father, Bebe was.

T.J. said, "You let her!"

How could I stop her? I said, "What's the big deal? It was just a joke."

T.J. said, "My dad's a cool guy and she made him out to be some sloppy old drunk or something."

"No she didn't," I said. "That's part of the joke to exaggerate. C'mon, honey."

T.J. said, "Oh well, I wouldn't have to exaggerate if I was doing her."

Then he doubled over and stuck his butt out as far as it could go, stuck his hands in his pocket and drew his pants skintight and started bumping and grinding. In a shrill voice he went, "How low can you go?"

"Uh-unnnn stop it," I said.

"That's what you should have told her," T.J. said.

"T.J.," I said, "you're making a mountain out of a molehill."

He said, "Your loud fat-butt friend started it."

Fat? Bebe is not fat, she's solid. I said, "Don't talk about her like that and she's not fat." Then I added, because I was mad, "If she was so distasteful, why was your father trying to hit on her?"

T.J. said, "She was flirting with him first!"

Please! Now I was steaming and I was throwing dish towels and plates into the sink.

T.J. leaned against the doorway and said, "And another thing. He had no business letting her win that dance contest either trying to be a gentleman."

I almost collapsed. Let her win? I looked T.J. dead in the eye. "She smoked him."

T.J. shook his head no.

I said again with attitude, "She smoked him and *then some* and even held back a taste."

T.J. had a dish in his hand and he intentionally let it go and it crashed against the floor.

"What's wrong with you?" I shouted. He must have lost his mind dropping my mama's good plate. I said again, "What's wrong with you?"

"It slipped," T.J. said sarcastically.

"Get out," I said.

T.J. folded his arms across his chest and leaned in the doorway as if to say, "Move me."

"Excuse me?" I said to him. "Excuse me, sir—I pay the bills here and I said get out!"

T.J. casually looked at his nails. I jerked around and grabbed the phone and dialed security. He jumped behind me and grabbed the phone out of my hand. He forced the phone back in the cradle on the wall and held my hands.

I jerked. "Let me go!"

T.J. kept going "Sssh!"

I spun around and he tried to put his fingers to my lips. I slapped his hand away.

T.J. pressed his fingers against his own lips and quieted, "Sssh!" His eyes pleaded and T.J. said, "Sorry-sorry-sorry."

I told him, "Yeah, you're sorry all right!"

I turned back around and clutched the sink. After a minute, I turned around to face him and T.J. was standing there looking determined.

"I don't want to leave like this," he said.

The argument was silly and had escalated unnecessarily. I told T.J. that I wasn't mad at Bebe for making fun of Speed. I was mad at him for being so damn sensitive over some childish B.S.

T.J. shrugged and gave in and he said, "We both were wrong—check that—we all had our moments tonight, why not leave it at that?"

That was lame and I almost told him so but I was tired of fighting. I'd had a hard day. I was emotionally drained and I didn't want any more stress. More fighting was just out with me. I said, "T.J., I just want to pretend that Bebe never made fun of your father, that you never made fun of her, and we never had this fight."

T.J. reached out and took my hand and kissed it. He said, "Daddy said you were classy."

I know he was trying to make it up to me by turning on the charm but that was a crutch and I didn't want to let him use that crutch on me. I said, "Un-huh." I know it sounded lame too but I was just worn out. T.J. took me in his arms and he hugged me. The last thing I wanted right now was sex. I was mentally and physically stalled.

"Sandy?" T.J. said.

I said, "T.J., I'm not . . ."

And he cut me off.

He said, "I just want to hold you. Can I hold you?"

And T.J. continued to hug me and then he walked me to the living room couch and we sat down and he sat back and I laid my head in his lap. T.J. massaged my temples with the tips of his fingers. And I just felt all that tension easing out of me. Just like a punctured tire loses air? That's how I felt. I could just feel all that tension draining out of me. Good-bye and good riddance. And I was glad it was leaving and even happier that it was by T.J.'s hands that I was getting relief.

The next couple of days went by and nothing special happened until Friday evening. I was in the office and Harvey walked in. Harvey was grinning from every part of his face. His eyes were grinning. His mouth was grinning. The wrinkles on his face were grinning too.

"Did you win the lotto?" I asked.

"Maybe," Harvey said.

I looked at him and said, "What's up?"

Harvey said, "I just met with the Standard Electric Company. Standard makes electrical appliances, like radios and televisions. Standard wants to be like General Electric and Westinghouse and get into the broadcasting business."

"You're selling?" I said.

"Not all of it—I'm going to sell them part of the company, keep majority interest, and use the money to pay for a new studio and equipment. But before they will talk cold deal I want to have a meeting and give a presentation from the sales department on this year's figures and projections."

Harvey grinned at me, then continued, "I want you to head the team that puts it together and I want you to give the actual presentation!"

Wow! This was a big deal. I mean this was important. I was excited that Harvey had that kind of confidence in me and at the same time I was a little nervous because it was such an important job.

Harvey must have sensed it because he said, "You'll handle it. I want to put Tia and Jackson on the team. Tia minored in accounting and she can crunch the numbers. Jackson has experience in graphics and he can take care of the charts and graphs."

The first thing that hit me was that Tia was kind of lazy. Don't get me wrong, she had good accounts, but if she applied herself she could have more. Tia just wasn't a hustler to me. We got along fine, but she didn't seem to have the edge that I like.

Should I say something? I didn't want to dog a sister out to the boss. And what would Harvey say if I did? He must not see her as I do or he wouldn't put her on the team. Would he think I was jealous of Tia? Would he think I was petty? And one sister dogging out another to the boss—a white male boss—didn't sit well with me. And I think that was the heaviest hand holding me. Why? If Tia were a white man, would I say something? If she were a white woman, would I say something? The odds were greater that I would. I just felt that as a black person I owed her no blockage. It was hard enough in the workplace to make it without someone . . . someone of your own race . . . blocking you. This was an opportunity for her. Was I afraid she'd outshine me? I thought a minute, but my gut said no.

So I smiled at Harvey and said, "Great, I'm ready."

Then Harvey dropped the bomb and said that it had to be done in two weeks. I said, "Two weeks!"

Harvey said, "I want to move fast and you know we're not the only radio station in town—there's a big bonus in it for you guys when it's over."

Later that night, I told T.J. about it and the first thing he said was, "That won't make you miss our brunch?"

I said, "No, it won't because the presentation's the day before."

Then T.J. said, "Good. Sounds like old Harvey's got a lot of faith in you."

"Yeah," I said, "and I don't want to let him down. He wants Tia and Jackson to work with me on preparing it."

T.J. said, "What will they do?"

And I told him that Tia had experience in accounting and Harvey wanted her to crunch the numbers and such. Jackson was really good with making charts and graphs. Of all the staff, the three of us were the team he felt would do the best job.

T.J. said, "What do you think?"

I told him, "Tia can be a little lazy, but I think we'll all rise to the occasion. We'll be fine."

t.j.

Obviously Sandy didn't know that Tia didn't like her. Sandy said they got along fine at work. Tia obviously had enough sense to keep her personal feelings out of business. But I didn't know if I should tell Sandy that Tia didn't care for her too much and to watch out for her, just on G.P. It was just a feeling I had. But how could I tell Sandy that without telling her how I knew?

I could say that when I was talking with Tia at the party that she'd said something derogatory . . . you know about her sucking up to the boss . . . but then Sandy would go to her with it. Then Tia might get pissed off and start blabbing about our little boot knocking—so I couldn't go that route.

I tried asking Sandy again about how she felt about Tia being on the project, and she said she's a little lazy but they get along fine. So she wasn't giving me any incident that I could pry open and say, "Oh, seems like she doesn't like you" or "Watch your back," or something like that. If I wanted to warn Sandy at all, at the very least, I'd have to tell her about that first night I had sex with Tia. And that was before Sandy and I started kicking it together, but she would still get pissed off about it. Oh, yeah. Sandy would get a world of attitude behind that.

Aww, I just needed to chill because I was probably making something out of nothing. I told myself, Chill, my brother! Sandy is tops at her job and she'll handle the project fine. I don't need to tell her a thing. Sandy will be fine. Plus, I've got my own worries. I'm worried about my brunch with Oscar Peterson.

Oscar Peterson is a legend. He's a big guy with massive hands and yet he has feathers for fingers. Touch. A piano is not all about notes. It's about touch. Two people can play the same song and it'll sound different because of touch. Touch dictates tempo and feeling. Peterson is the touch master. Even after he had that stroke, he's still the touch master.

Meeting him will be a once-in-a-lifetime deal. It was very cool of my boy to include me in. I'm sure going to take a tape of my music. I hope he won't think that's too forward. Yeah, he might. Maybe what I'll do is get real cool with him at brunch, then ask him if I can send it to him. Naw, he's got an agent and a publicist, I'm sure, and they'll run interference. Peterson will never get it. I'll just have to think of something cool to say or no, no, I'll get Sandy to do it.

My girl can pull it out and say like, "Oh, here, I want you to hear T.J.'s work!"

Then I'll act like I'm mad and say something like, "Aww, don't impose like that on Mr. Peterson."

And then Sandy'll say something like, "Don't be mad. I'm just trying to help you. You're great."

Then Oscar Peterson will take the tape.

Yeah, that's cool. That's how we'll play it. I gotta tell Sandy. We'll need to run through it a couple of times to make sure it sounds and plays right. Yeah, cool.

speed

Good God Almighty! That Crown Royal is pistol-whipping my head from the inside out. I was swinging at Players last night. What time did I quit stepping? Two? Three? Four? My toes are burning now. The devil is dancing now. He's dancing with the bottom of my feet; flames and pitchforks bopping with my heels and toes. That's what Mama used to say when I was young and wouldn't—naw, check that—couldn't get up for church on Sunday morning.

She'd say, "The devil got a hold of them big, nasty feet and won't let go! He done hobbled you and your daddy good for dancing with him instead of God!"

Daddy would yell from his bed, "Leave the boy alone!"

Mama would quietly put on a Sunday hat and stroll out the front door. Mama and those hats! Oooooh-wee! Blue velvet with white feather borders. Yellow brims, broke down over the eye. Pastel pillboxes with web veils. Mama went to church with a sanctified spirit wearing Holy Ghost headgear. I just knew she was the prettiest angel flitting around here on earth and I'd slop them covers over my head and yell out to Daddy. I'd always have to yell two or three times, 'cause I had been out with him and he was worse off than me!

"Daddy," I'd yell out.

He'd grunt back.

I'd say, "We going to hell!"

And Daddy would smack his lips together, snort, and say, "Not if your ma can help it—she'll pray us in on layaway!"

I laughed now like I laughed then! Heaven on layaway!

I should get up. It's after eleven and I should get up and eat. Most folks can't dance and drink all night and then get up and eat some bacon, eggs, and cheese grits. I can. I can eat. Hangovers leave me with a headache and an appetite too. Shine used to make me bacon, eggs, cheese grits, and French toast. French toast is still T.J.'s favorite.

He'd sit on the countertop, his little Pro-Keds doing an old soft shoe against the metal cabinet. That boy had music in him from the get-go. He'd beat the eggs, hitting the spoon against the sides of the glass dish, and accompany it with that old soft shoe. Shine? She'd hum. It wasn't no monkey business or mistake. They had talent together.

I remember that first breakfast after she died. My mama came over and she woke me up. I must have had three bottles of whatever it was in the liquor cabinet. I woke up with my head damn near about to fall off and boy was I hungry. I managed somehow to stagger to the table. The inside of my mouth was bland and my stomach was growling. T.J. was standing there in his pajamas. There were unicorns on them. Blue. Green. Red. Unicorns. Faded unicorns.

Mama said, "Sit down, baby, and Grandma will fix your favorite, French toast."

Now mind you, I'd sat up with T.J. the night before. I let him cry himself to sleep, then I commenced to drinking myself to sleep. I said, "Ma, let T.J. fix the eggs. That boy can beat some eggs." And T.J.? Not a word. He just stood there chewing on the insides of his mouth. Chewing. But no sound.

I was sitting at the table. My head was pounding and my stomach was growling and my crotch was itching and I was scratching 'neath the table on the sly and trying to smile for my mama and my boy.

And Ma gave T.J. a spoon, his bowl, an egg, and said, "Crack the egg, baby."

T.J. stared at it and squeezed it—cracked it right in his hand!

Ma was shocked, then she wiped his hand with her apron and kissed him. T.J. started crying softly. I just buried my head in the crook of my elbow and held the tears in. When I could manage my insides, I scooped him up in my lap and we hugged each other tight. When Mama put that French toast in front of us, I ate and T.J. did too.

From that day on for near 'bout, oh I'd say, let's see, maybe two years Mama or Shine's girlfriends from church or our neighbors would cook our meals. They would come to the door, ring the bell, and say they made too much oxtail soup or chicken and dumplings or had a couple of extra sweet-potato pies. These ladies would come and hug on T.J. and fix his plate and ask him about school. He was the only child in the neighborhood who didn't have a mama at home and I think everybody else wanted to be his mama and take up Shine's slack. They sent T.J. to the store to get little stuff they didn't need just so they could give him some money. These ladies took to tellin' T.J. how cute he was and told him to make sure he practiced that piano 'cause the talent he had wasn't no toy and he should be dead serious with it. T.J. used to say, "Boy, Daddy, the ladies sure do love us!"

I'd tell him, "Yes they do!"

And they did, God bless 'em! It gave them joy to do for us because they missed Shine and I thought it was a testament to Shine's personality that so many folks wanted to help the one and only child she left behind.

T.J. called and told me about this idea he has about slipping a sample of his music to this Peterson guy at brunch. It sounds cool to me, so I told him to ask Sandy and to make sure they're smooth about it. Ain't nothing worse than trying to play something off and it comes off ragged.

bebe

Sandy was working so hard on her presentation that whenever I called my homette, she was stressed. So I decided to surprise her one night. I went over to her house with some Chinese food. Sandy loves Chinese food. I took her some egg rolls, shrimp egg foo yung, and some pepper steak. We broke out the plates and the chopsticks and started to grub on down. When we finished, we both stretched out on the rug and chatted there for a minute.

Sandy said, "Bebe—Hypothetical."

Sandy does that, see, we play a game sometimes and ask each other make-believe questions to see what the other person will say. Hypothetical, Be. I said, "Okay, shoot."

Sandy said, "You're married . . ."

I cut her off and said, "Is he rich and handsome?"

Sandy rushed on, "Yeah."

"Make him real, then," I laughed.

Sandy swatted me with a pillow. "Pay attention, girl." Sandy went on, "You're at home in bed after a hard week and he comes in in a good mood and wants to make love. Do you (A) tell him no and promise to make it up to him later? Do you (B) go ahead and try to rise to the occasion and satisfy him even though you are not in the mood? Or do you (C) go ahead and fake it so you can hurry up and get back to sleep?"

I had to ask her, "Where did you get that one?"

She said one of her coworkers had asked a similar question at lunch.

"Who?" I asked, because we both were familiar with each

other's coworkers from talking to each other about our jobs so much.

Sandy said, "Melissa."

Melissa? Dawg, she just got married. Sandy nodded, then cut her eyes with a smile: which one?

I said, "(D) I'll call you to come over as a fill-in."

We laughed a little bit and Sandy said sarcastically, "I'm not home."

I was just clowning. I knew which one I would pick and that would be A.

Sandy grinned. "That's what I thought you would say."

I said, "Why?"

Sandy said, "You're the type of person who is up front about what she feels and who doesn't seem to be afraid of conflict but yet you want to be liked."

Uhh-aaah, okay. That was a fair read. But I know Sandy as well as she knows me. I knew which one Sandy would pick. I asked her, "Which would you choose?"

Sandy said without hesitation, "A."

I looked at her cockeyed and said, "Go away, little girl!"

Sandy got loud and indignant with it. "A."

"Sandy," I said, "you know good and well you wouldn't pick A!"

"Why not?" Sandy said.

I told her, "You hate conflict and will bend over backwards to please other people not to have conflict. I think you'd go along and just fake it just so as not to piss the man off and hurt his feelings—that's C. A lot of times you put the feelings of others in front of your own wants and desires."

"I do not," she said.

"Do too."

"Do not."

"Do too."

It was getting a little serious and I got up on my knees and put my hands on my hips like a little kid. "Do too—do too—do too!" Then I stuck out my tongue. "Nah!"

Sandy dismissed me with an underhanded wave. She said sarcastically, "I'll 'C' you."

I just shrugged and thought to myself, "A" my butt!

sandy

T.J. knew that I was working on getting my project together. I was pulling all kind of crazy hours and stuff. He called and said that he wanted me to give Oscar Peterson his tape at brunch. He told me how and that was fine but then T.J. said he wanted to practice. What was this, a TV drama? T.J. was more nervous and excited about this than I was about my project!

That may be because the project is going so well. Tia and Jackson have been great. Everything I've asked them to do they've done well and fast. I've been going through our account listings and budget gross records from last quarter and Tia has been checking figures and Jackson has been working on the graphs. For a small radio station, we're damn strong in the market. I needed to practice my presentation, what I would say, tone, eye contact, and all that. T.J. was bugging me about coming over and practicing this tape handoff.

"It's not the NFL, T.J.," I said. "Relax."

One night he just showed up at my place and I was dead-tired but he looked so fine. He had a bottle of champagne in one hand and a bunch of wax balloons in the other hand. On the balloons it said, "You're number 1!"

"Practice?" he said. "We'll do mine, then do yours, how about it?"

We did his but when my turn came, tired as I was, I was ready for something else. Being around T.J. just did something to me.

I undressed him by slipping the sweater up and I stopped when his chest was exposed and kissed him there. I pulled the sweater over his head and our mouths met, open and dry and dying for a taste of each other. T.J. was warm and exciting. I liked that. I liked handling him because where I touched gave generously.

When I circled my arms around his shoulders and caressed his back, I was greedy and just couldn't get enough and I found myself squeezing, trying to squeeze all the sex out of him until he was a helpless set of bones wobbling around in my embrace. I whispered in his ear what I wanted and he eagerly agreed. T.J. was a yes-man.

I felt his limbs and they were all strong, energetic, sweaty, and desirous. Our bodies were swelling all over the place and I felt the insides of my legs smart from our friction until we got a rhythm that allowed us to melt into each other. That's when it really gets good. There's just one continuous flow and I felt like I was sailing and I know I wasn't going anywhere but yet I was moving emotionally and I couldn't help but talk in sexual tongue, language that only made sense when our physical selves went haywire. When it was over, T.J. didn't want to leave. And I didn't want him to either. We spent the entire night together.

The closer it got to the date of the presentation, the more T.J. and Bebe would call and give me pep talks and encouragement. I knew we were ready. I had my notes in my computer at work and a hard copy at home. The last time T.J. called he wanted to make sure that everything was still cool for brunch. It was going to be the day after my presentation. I was glad it wasn't before because I wouldn't have been able to enjoy it. This way after the presentation I could go home and crash and relax until the brunch. And I'd either have two good days or one bad day and one good day. I couldn't see how anything could go wrong at the brunch.

The day of my presentation I woke up at about five-thirty in the morning. Way too early. I tried to go back to sleep but my body wasn't cooperating. It wanted to do its own thing, so I got up and turned on the tube and checked out CNN for a while. But the news was so bad that it rattled me more than anything else. I had to turn that stuff off. So I decided to have a big breakfast and then just go in early. We'd said to be in at nine to go over everything one last time before the meeting at ten. I made some pancakes, eggs, and turkey sausage. I hadn't had a breakfast like that since the last time I had the flu. But it was cold out and snowing and a heavy meal would make me feel better I figured. So after eating I felt good and I took a shower. I was feeling better and better.

I started thinking about the bonus and what I wanted to spend it on after I put some money into my savings account. I started layering down with clothes. I warmed up the car and I just couldn't get over how confident I felt. How powerful I felt. I could make or break this deal. I was in control and in charge. I was hot. Harvey knew it. The more I thought about what was ahead, the more I looked forward to it. I was ready to showcase myself. I was going to be *on*.

I got to the office at about eight. I was taking my stuff off and I saw a light on under my door, which was slightly ajar. Maybe I'd forgotten to turn off the light. I pushed the door open and Tia was sitting at my desk, with my computer on, deleting files. I stood and watched her for a moment so there was no mistake. I was stunned. I was confused. Finally I snapped out of it and said, "What the hell are you doing?"

I know it's an old saying, but she did—she did—almost jump out of her skin. Tia's eyes were big and I could see her chest jerking as she tried to catch her breath.

She said, "Oh, you scared me."

Scared her? Of course, it was obvious that she wasn't expecting me. She tried to turn off the computer and I grabbed her hand.

I said, "You're in my files and I saw you deleting them!"

Tia shook her head no.

I was so angry that I said, "Bullshit!"

That's what I said and I don't like to curse but I told Tia that straight to her face. Then I could tell that she was starting to get her bearings. She started to think.

I said, "Why?"

Tia said, "Because you think you're better than me."

"How is that?" I asked her. "I've always treated you nicely in every way."

Tia said, "You put on airs and want to be the only star in sales. The only reason that you have the top spot is because you kiss Harvey's ass."

This girl had lost her mind. I picked up the phone and said, "Well, let's see if Harvey wants you to keep your job after this!"

And Tia said, "Fine—I might lose my job but you're not tops over me in everything—not in sex."

I stopped dialing.

Tia said, "I fucked T.J. and he said I was twice as good as you, so, Miss Thang, you can't have too many airs because your man is stepping out on you."

She's lying! That was my first thought that she was lying. Tia saw it in my eyes and she started to describe T.J.'s house and the curtains that I had just picked out with the little pianos around the border. Tia described the creaky steps, the narrow old-fashioned windows, and then she reached in her purse and pulled out a magnet I had seen on T.J.'s refrigerator.

Tia said, "I knew I might need it one day when I let you know and I needed proof."

Then she told me about a little splotch of a birthmark that he had. I'd noticed it. Only his parents and his lovers could describe it. That started my head to splitting and I reached for somewhere to sit down but there was nowhere. I heard her say if I call Harvey she'll call me a lie and that she'll say that I was trying to set her up because she was going out with T.J.

I managed to mumble, "When?"

183

Tia said, "The last time we got together was after the Matador when you left him hanging! But that doesn't matter because, you know, I had him first! The very night of the sales party. He came over to my place late and we made love. He thought I didn't see him take the phone in the bathroom and make a call. But, hey, after he left I hit the redial button and it was you. I recognized your voice."

I remembered the call that I thought was a wrong number at the time. Now my head was really hurting.

Tia hovered over me and asked repeatedly, "What are you going to do?"

What was I going to do? I was going to get out of there. I had a volcanic pain bubbling in the narrow part of my chest. I was hurt and angry and I wanted to get out of there. I got up and walked for my coat. Then I stopped. What about the presentation? How could I give it with my head spinning? I would have no balance of thought; no focus of goal. Tia and T.J. had already beat me down personally. I didn't need to let them kill me professionally too. I grabbed my coat.

Tia said, "Where are you going?"

I told her, "You want to be a star, so here's your chance. You give the presentation."

Then I put my coat on and walked out. The cold air smacked me in the face but I just ducked my head and plowed forward toward the parking lot. How could he do this? I had done so much for him. I'd given him money. I'd given him time. I'd given him encouragement. I'd given him affection and sex. What could T.J. want with a whore like Tia? She had no class. She was evil and sneaky and a dirty, rotten dog. And he just had to get with her. Tia of all people. And she had a big mouth. I know she told some of the girls in the office. And here I'd bragged about T.J. and they all looked like oh yeah he sounds great and they were probably laughing at me! I was so embarrassed. I could feel my face getting hotter and hotter and my nose started running and I had tissue in my purse but I just wiped my nose with my coat sleeve. I just wanted to get in my car and go home. How could I give a presentation? My mind was ripped to pieces. My thoughts were all over the place.

I don't remember how I got home. The next thing I remember is lying across the bed and sobbing. I sounded like a kid. When you're a kid and you cry so hard and long that you start to hiccup? That's where I was.

I wanted to kick myself. I knew he was doggish. I knew that he thought he was a player. Why was I so upset? Why didn't I see that he couldn't hold it but for so long? I guess I thought that I could make him different. I thought that he would be different with me. I would even venture to say that in the back of my mind, not too far back, I had rationalized that if I found out he was still stepping out I would be prepared because it would be someone I didn't know, some ugly faceless nobody. I thought I could handle that if it came up.

But Tia? He knew that we worked together. He knew that Tia was real to me. Tia had told people at the office, I know! He embarrassed me! T.J. showed me no respect. Now every time I see her face I'll think of the betrayal. T.J. just let me have it! Blam! Right in the face. I looked at the clock and it was nine-thirty and I rolled over and grabbed the phone. I called and talked to Harvey's secretary. I told her that I was sick. Then I called Bebe.

bebe

When I got up this morning, I was feeling great. I'd found a new hairdresser who paid his taxes and who could get all that red shit out of my hair. And ya know, it was good to be my old, fine self again. I got to work and there were about ten people waiting outside in all this cold weather and snow. That happened around the first of the month. Folks armed with checks just couldn't wait. I saw Bernadette in the crowd and I waved at her. Anyway, I went in to open up and all the girls clapped. They were being smart-asses because I got my hair back together. I got a sense of humor. I put my hands on my hips and did my Patti LaBelle strut with attitude. We opened up and folks started coming in and I was working at the specialty section and did some savings bonds and opened a money market account. Bernadette came and slung her burlap sack of change on the counter. I asked about her little girl. Bernadette said she was with her grandmother for the week because she was on vacation from school. The look of freedom and pleasure on that woman's face! I started pouring her change into the counter when my line rang. It was Sandy. I knew it was her by the slow catch and drag in her voice. My first thought? She fucked up the presentation. How could she? She had practiced it for days! Then I glanced at the clock and saw that there was no way she could be through. That really scared me.

"What's wrong, Sandy?" I said into the phone.

And everything just started pouring out about Tia and the files and her sleeping with T.J. Sandy said she was so upset that she ended up walking out of the office.

I said, "T.J. did that?" Then I added, "That no-piano-playing motherfucker!"

Bernadette was still standing there. I knew she heard me and that was unprofessional. I told Sandy to give me ten minutes and I'd call her back at home. I hung up and started finishing with Bernadette and I told Robert that he needed to take over for me for a few minutes.

Bernadette asked, "What's wrong?"

I said, "My best friend is going out with this guy and he just dogged her out."

Bernadette said, "I'm not trying to be nosy but did you say T.J.?"

I nodded and she asked was he a musician and I said, "Yeah, he is." Then I described him.

Bernadette said, "Huh."

I said, "C'mon, so you know him, what's up?"

She hesitated and said she didn't want to get into nobody else's business; that's how people ended up in the graveyard. I promised her that it wouldn't be nothing like that. Sandy was my best friend and I needed to know. Plus, I added, I'd been giving her a break on the fee for counting this change and she owed me. She got the message. I took care of her business and told her to meet me in the rest room so we could talk.

When I got to the ladies' room, Bernadette started telling me about how T.J. came into Arturo's, where she worked a few months ago. Said she knew him from a couple of other bars she worked at. Bernadette said she knew his name and that he was a musician but that he never tried to hit on her or nothing. She just knew of him. Bernadette said he came in and was waiting on somebody when this woman named Mikki Duveaux came in.

I said, "The real estate Duveaux?"

She nodded and said, "She came in and threw a fit on T.J. because he owed her some money. Big money. Girl, she threw a

187

pitcher of water in his face and started beating his ass with it. She got so upset that she fainted! And the piano man—he blew her off just as cool. Then the Negro had the balls to give me ten dollars to shut up when his other woman came in."

That was Sandy! Sandy had told me the same incident except it had a whole other swing on it.

Bernadette said, "Your friend was in the car with you a little while back?"

I said, "Yeah."

I didn't even remember seeing Bernadette that day because I was so wired about my test and the return of Dap. But Bernadette said she thought she recognized Sandy in the car but she didn't say anything because if you don't start nothing, it won't be nothing.

Whoa! I went and called Sandy. I told her that I would take an early lunch and that I would be over there and I'd talk to her then. Then I asked her did she have T.J.'s soc-number? Sandy was like why? I told her I just wanted to check on something. I knew she'd been paying some of his bills. Sandy didn't want to get up and check, so I just nagged and nagged her until she did. Sandy kept good records, I knew that from doing her taxes. Sandy came back with the soc-number and I said, "Cool—just take a nap 'til I get there."

Sandy sniffled, "Okay."

I ran a credit check on that Negro.

At lunchtime, I drove over to Sandy's place. I was glad that my car was back up and running. I was going to get rid of this lemonade wagon when I got my next raise. Anyway, Sandy came to the door and she looked sad as a kid with no Christmas toy. When Sandy falls, she stone drops through the floor. She was walking around in just her full black slip and wasn't saying much, just mumbling.

"Coffee?" she asked.

"Naw, tea," I said.

Sandy just dragged her feet along the carpet, no slippers, and mumbled. She gave me a condensed version of the morning's events on the phone. Now I got the long version. This Tia chick was a crafty bitch. Sounded like she could cut your heart out and eat a Whopper at the same time.

But the girl ain't make T.J. go to bed with her, so I told Sandy, "Hey, don't blame it all on her."

Sandy just looked at me with burgundy bloodshot eyes. We came out of the kitchen and she just sat on the floor, on some pillows by the stereo, and I coped a squat there too. I asked her what she was feeling. I knew, but saying your pain is like throwing up—it's uncomfortable but it gets the bad stuff out.

Sandy said, "I feel like a fool and I feel mad and stupid and silly and I want to knock his block off."

She was taking this therapy well. She sipped on her coffee and I could smell that she had spiked it. Heavy.

I said, "Go light."

Sandy snapped back, "I'll go how I wanna go."

Ohhhhh-kay. She wanted to lash out and I knew how she felt. I'd gotten stepped on before. Hell, danced on. What am I saying, stomped on. I know it hurts and the longer you hold it in, the longer it will fester and grow. I asked her had she talked to T.J. and she said she hadn't had the energy to call him. What would she say? Then I watched Sandy start to rationalize.

She said, "Maybe I didn't do something. There's something I didn't do for him."

Hell, looked like Sandy did everything but birth the boy. What more could she have done? I listened to her beat herself up for a while. I should of spent more time with him. I should of gone with him to the club and he'd never would of run into Tia again. She threw all the maybes, could-haves, should-haves, and wish-I-hadas into the air. All that mess tossed together made not one good reason for T.J. acting a fool on her. Period.

I had to tell her. I didn't want to add to her misery and God knows I didn't want to tell her and hurt her anymore. Anybody who knows me knows that. But I had to let her know there was a pattern going on here. This wasn't about Sandy. It was about T.J. I told her about Bernadette and what really happened at Arturo's that day. Sandy looked more disappointed than shocked or angry.

Then I pulled out the credit check that I'd run on T.J. That boy had debts like you wouldn't believe. His credit was a wreck. He had monster credit card bills and all that. Then I outlined in red a personal loan from Friendly American Bank. It was for five thousand. When I first saw that, I put two and two together with the story Bernadette told me and I called one of my friends over at Friendly American. She looked it up and they'd given T.J. a personal loan for five g's and Miss Duveaux had cosigned for it. That's what the fight had been about. Sandy just dropped her head. I was mad. Damn mad at T.J. But you know, getting mad doesn't make you feel better. You get no consolation or satisfaction out of it. Sandy wasn't saying anything, she was just clenching and unclenching her fist.

"Mad?" I asked her.

Sandy nodded.

"Super-duper mad?" I asked her.

Sandy nodded harder.

"Pissed all the way off?" I asked her.

Sandy's hair just went to flying she was nodding so tough. I leaned in and talked so my words were a landslide tumbling down into her ear, "So what are you gonna do about it?"

She shrugged and her head bobbed and rolled slack on her neck. She was melting under the atomic heat of her own anger. Sandy needed to be saved or she was going to go splat! I knew a way to save her but she had to help save herself.

I asked my homette, "So what are you going to do about T.J.?"

Sandy moved away from me, trying to unlock our handcuff gaze. No dice. And she was still clenching her fists. I was on her.

"Aren't you tired?" I said. "Look like you ought to be a little bit tired. C'mon, it's human nature to want to get somebody back. What? Are you from Saturn or somewhere? Is there a ring around your head—a halo you think maybe?"

That got her to sit up.

She zinged me, "Shut up, Be, don't you see I don't want to be bothered with some silly shit?"

Yeah, I could see that. But hell, T.J. shouldn't get away with the mess he was pulling. Why? Why let him pimp away untouched? What was up with that?

I said, "Don't get mad—get even!"

Sandy waved me off, "Go on, Bebe."

Go on what?

"Stop being so prissy," I told her.

Sandy needed to stop trying to prove that she was above everybody. Her friends, family, and T.J. too all knew she had class. She didn't have to fight natural instinct, be a doormat to prove it. It was like being a kid and being picked on: you wanted to hit back at least once even though you had already gotten your butt kicked. Ya felt better. Ya had more respect for yourself.

I reasoned with her, "Do something to fuck with his mind like he fucked with yours. We can figure something out that will get on his last nerve! That's all I'm speaking on."

Sandy mumbled a weak no, then slammed her hand against the table and shouted, "I'm not getting into any of that ghetto stuff— cutting up clothes and slashing tires."

Ghetto? Hey, I told her, I didn't have a ghetto brain cell in my head. "Excuse me," I said, "I'm talking about doing something scientifically low-down that we can laugh about later. Don't wait to exhale, breathe, damn it!"

Sandy stared at me and then busted out laughing. She was snorting and everything. Watching her, I got tickled too.

Sandy finally got herself together after a minute. "Okay, Be. Let's put on our thinking caps, huh?"

forty-nine

sandy

Don't get mad, get even. Breathe. Scientifically low-down. That's what Bebe said. She told me to think about it and she'd see me after work. All I wanted to do was sleep. Misery was always a sleeping pill for me. Holding negative stuff in made me tired. It settled along my eyelids and put sleeping powder in my eyes. I lay down and the phone rang. I answered it and it was Harvey. He sounded very alarmed because his secretary told him that I'd gone home sick with the flu. Harvey said he knew if I wasn't there today I must be near death. That confidence made me smile. Then the smile left me because I'd dropped the ball and let a screwup like Tia pick it up. But don't you know Harvey said she did a good job? He said he was surprised but everything went great. Harvey said things looked super and that it couldn't have been done without me.

Harvey laughed and said, "Bonus time! When will you be back to work?"

I said, "A few days."

And Harvey was so cool about it that after hanging up I felt bad about lying. But what other choice did I have? Couldn't tell Harvey about Tia. No way. And before Bebe left I told her that I was thinking about quitting and getting another job.

And Bebe said, "I know you not gonna quit that good job over some bullshit?"

How was I supposed to work with Tia? Huh? How could I look at her every day? I knew in my gut that I couldn't. I had hoped that she would fail. Wished it. Did everything but pray it. But no

192

dice. Tia came out like a champ. She'd made two knocks today. But it wasn't like I was going to starve or something. I'd already had two job offers before, one from an all-news station and the other from an adult contemporary station. Both were in the top five in Arbitron ratings and that translated into bigger sales and easier sales. The latter sounded good. I really didn't want to leave J-108 but like the song says, everything must change.

The next call I got was from T.J. I let the answering machine pick up. The message was in that sexy tone and he said, "Hey, babe, it's T.J. calling to hear your great news about killing them in that meeting today—I'm thinking bonus and Bahamas—talk to you soon."

As the message was playing I was yelling at the answering machine. I yelled, "Dog! Asshole!"

That's the kind of stuff I was yelling and I felt the bottom of my lip trembling. I thought about what Bebe said about not getting mad but to concentrate on getting even.

Why not? I was feeling better about letting her talk me into getting T.J. back. Maybe I was too conservative. I'd always been a Goody Two-Shoes. I never cut class. I never took a piece of bubble gum out of the store that didn't belong to me. I'd been in the national honor society—no drugs or alcohol or smoking ever in high school. I'd gotten a scholarship to college and still no drugs and I wasn't wild or evil or mean and I treated people how I would like to be treated. And what had it gotten me in the way of romance? What did Montel Williams' bald head look like? A big round zero.

T.J. called two more times and I just turned down the answering machine. He was the last person I wanted to talk to. I kept thinking about getting him back. Now Bebe had given me a seed and it was sprouting awhile in my brain. Why not mess with him? What was the harm in letting him know that he hurt me and I didn't like it? I was surprised myself that Bebe had talked me into this because it wasn't like me. But deep down inside I wanted to pop him upside his head and say, "Wake up, stupid!" And I truly think a wake-up call from me would throw something heavy on his mind.

When Bebe made it back over, she brought shrimp fried rice, cashew chicken, and beef and broccoli. I'd told her that I wasn't hungry.

And Bebe cracked, "You too skinny now!"

And she knew I loved Chinese, so I had to have some and I did feel better after I'd eaten. Bebe asked had I come up with an idea on what to do about T.J. I told her no not really but I wasn't about to do anything too crazy but I definitely wanted to do something.

Bebe said, "Cool, I got an idea. Tell me, what is closest to his heart?"

I said, "Seems like his penis."

Bebe hunched her eyebrows up and down and said, "Wanna be in *Jet* as the black Lorena Bobbitt?" And she held her chopsticks like daggers. We smiled and Bebe said, "You get my meaning— but for real, something important to him."

"I-I don't know, Be," I moaned.

Bebe wiggled her eyebrows up and down and said, "We need some musical inspiration." She held up this tape she had brought with her, went over to the stereo, and put it on. "Stylistics," she said. And they started singing that payback is a dog! Bebe can give you drama twenty-four hours a day! Then I thought of something. I told Bebe and she said it was a start and that we'd refine it, come up with a plan, and execute it.

t.j.

I was calling and calling and calling Sandy. I wanted to hear how her presentation went. I know she got down. They all probably went out somewhere and were celebrating or something. I also wanted to double-check our brunch date tomorrow. I wanted Sandy to pick me up at about nine, brunch was at ten. It was kind of funny that we both were going to have big days back-to-back. But it was kind of funky that she hadn't called yet to tell me about her big day, and I had invited her to share in mine. But I guess she was out and just excited about getting it over with.

It was hard getting through the day because I was so anxious about the brunch. I stopped by Players and saw Daddy and he was chilling with a brew. Miss Ann was there sipping on her Diet Coke. Outlaw was in the back cussing folks out. The usual. I went to bed early just like I used to do as a kid. Before birthdays. Before Christmas. Before graduation. I was always of the mind that the day would get there quicker that way. I left a message on Sandy's machine about what time to pick me up. She could have called back. Was she ignoring me? Naw, Sandy was taking care of business. They were probably out wining and dining those new investors. So I turned in and slept well, but I did have this dream.

I saw just a film, like lace, but with different colors. It was flowing as if a nice little breeze was whipping it around. Each time it came closest to my vision the color changed. The last color was black and then that black turned into a piano and I could see myself sitting down to play. There was cheering, deafening cheering, as I sat down. When I started to play, every key I touched turned into gold. No kidding. And the cheering got louder and louder. Finally the entire piano turned into solid gold. I hated that my alarm woke me up.

I bummed around and got in the shower and took a nice hot one. It was a cold snowy morning and I didn't want to catch a chill. The last thing I needed was a cold. I got dressed and it was about eight-thirty. I was anxious. I heard a horn honk and I went to the window and looked out—it wasn't Sandy. But I looked and I saw this big white thing in front of the door.

I opened the door and there was this big mound of melting snow. I mean it was high. It was at the top of my chest. Think of a snowman but just a solid block of snow just piled up higher and higher. I could see the edge of the sky around the doorway but I couldn't get out. It was too much snow and it was too solid. What the hell? Then I saw a purple envelope with my name on it stuck near the top. I opened it and it said, "Here's a block of ice for a cold motherfucker." Then it said, "P.S.—You had to fuck Tia, huh?" Damn! I was busted! Sandy knew. That bigmouth Tia had to flap her gums! And look at all this snow. I couldn't get out the door! The snow was solid. I grabbed the phone and called Sandy.

She picked up and I said, "What the hell—"

Sandy said, "Go to hell!" And hung up.

I'm yelling, "Sandy! Sandy!"

I dialed again, real slow. Same thing. She was messing me up! That bigmouth Tia! That bitch! Fine, I needed to stay calm. I didn't want to miss the brunch, so I decided to go out the back door and catch a cab a couple of blocks up. Maybe by the time I got back the stuff would be melted. I got to the back door and I pulled but it wouldn't open. I was pulling with all my weight and it wasn't budging. What to do? I looked through the little window and there was no snow. It must be jammed, so I pulled again. I looked out the window again. This time I saw a little squirt gun and empty canisters lying all around. Liquid Nails construction glue. I started pulling and pulling at the door! Sandy didn't do this shit by herself. That bitch Bebe was in on it. Sandy didn't have it in her to be real evil. But big-butt Bebe? This was her M.O.

I slammed my fist against the door. How was I going to get out? I couldn't go out the front window or the bedroom windows. The house was ninety-six years old and it has those narrow crank windows. I could look at them and tell I wasn't gonna fit. Now time was flying and I was gonna miss brunch. That's what they wanted. Sandy and Bebe were trying to derail my program. They wanted to nuke my big day. Sandy knew how to get back, yeah she came up with something crazy devious all right. But I wasn't about to be outdone! Oh, hell no!

I ran upstairs to the attic. The window up there was wider and I could fit out of it. I piled up some of the crates with my tapes in them and stood on top. I opened the window and looked down. Man, it was a long drop! Even if I made a rope out of sheets, it was dangerous. Suppose I fell? I could get knocked out and no-body would know. I would be lying out in this cold weather un-conscious or with broken bones—I could hurt my hands. Aww, naw! Damn her!

Now I was trying to think. What, what now? Boom! Call Daddy. I bolted back downstairs and phoned him. Daddy doesn't like to be called this early but it was an emergency and he would just have to get over it. He was all groggy and stuff and I had to yell into the phone to get him to snap out of it. I told him I was trapped in the house and he needed to come over and help me. It was an emergency and hurry up. I hung up the phone and I was just so pissed! I walked around kicking stuff, pillows and chairs, and I slammed my hands down on the keyboard. My piano screamed out in frustration for me. Sometimes life is too hard, you know?

speed

The boy woke me up before eleven o'clock. I don't like getting up out of my bed before eleven o'clock on *any day*, plus I've been dragging a little bit for a couple of weeks now. But I had to get up. My son was talking all crazy about being trapped in the house. What kind of mess was that? But he was so wild talking and excited I had to get up and go. I swung by and got Outlaw too. Three heads was better than one, particularly when two were mine and Outlaw's. Anyway, we drove up to the house, and there was this big glob of snow in front of the door. We just stood and looked at it for a minute. I tightened my scarf and said, "Damn, Outlaw, that's tripped out, huh?"

Outlaw nodded, "Yeah, real tripped out!" Then he smiled and we both started cracking up.

T.J. cranked open the front window and yelled, "C'mon and get me out of here!"

Me and Outlaw locked shoulders and walked up on the porch and we talked to T.J. through the window.

"Man," Outlaw said, "I'm glad I don't mess with these young slices, they too devious."

"What did you do?" I asked T.J.

He started yelling, "Never mind, get me out."

Well, I told him to go out the back door and then he explained about the Liquid Nails construction glue. Me and Outlaw went around the back and saw the canisters and stuff.

"How'd she know about that stuff?" Outlaw asked.

T.J. said, "Her daddy was a construction worker!"

Yep! That Liquid Nails ain't nothing to play with. Wasn't no way to just pull that door open. I looked from the outside and she'd saturated all around the cracks in the door and the screws! You'd have to get tools and rip the whole door off. T.J. had to go to that brunch and I knew it was important to him.

"Call the fire department," I reasoned.

Outlaw said, "That'll take too long."

"No, they'll get here quick," I said.

"I can dig T.J. out before the fire department can get here," Outlaw said.

Bullshit! I looked at Outlaw like he was crazy. Ya know, Outlaw always did try to go for bad.

He was snotty when he said, "You don't think so?"

I knew not! I tried to give him his props by reasoning.

I said, "I'm just saying, Outlaw, why go to all that trouble when our tax dollars pay the fire department?"

Outlaw knew I didn't believe him.

He pointed to the garage. "Get me a shovel and a pick."

I got the tools and we went back to the front of the house.

T.J. yelled, "Hurry up, shit!"

"Did you hear that?" I asked Outlaw. "I know he ain't cuss at us."

Outlaw nodded yep.

I told T.J., "You'd better cool out, Mr. Freeze, or we'll leave your ass up in there!"

Outlaw laughed and T.J. calmed down a little bit. You know he was hopping around like when he was a kid and had to go to the bathroom. Outlaw leaned on his shovel and grabbed his nuts and surveyed the job. I checked it out too and it was a big job. And it was getting hard like ice. T.J. started banging on the window again. I wished he'd go somewhere and sit down. Let the old heads handle everything.

I said, "Player, if your game was tight you wouldn't be in such bad shape, so cop a squat, please."

Outlaw leaned over to the window and said, "T.J., you lucky

I'm here 'cause your daddy would waste a whole lot of time waiting on the fire department, but I'm a take-charge guy. I'll have you out in twenty minutes!"

"Man, are you crazy?" I asked. I thumped that mound of snow and ice and told that fool, "Impossible."

"Wanna bet?" Outlaw said.

I said, "Cool."

Outlaw said, "Fifty?"

T.J. said something and I told him to shut up. I thumped that snow and ice again and said, "Go hard or go home, player!"

That made Outlaw mad! He got mad whenever I tried to say that he was half-stepping about something.

"Call it," he said.

"Bet my tab?" I said.

Outlaw's eyes went Buckwheat. My tab was hellified. But you know I wasn't about to lose. Outlaw was determined. I checked my watch for a clear start. Outlaw bent down.

I said, "On your mark, get set . . ." and my man Outlaw was gone.

That first stab, I heard that crunching sound and I had to jump back. Outlaw gave three more quick stabs and got a little break. He started scooping and heaving snow over his shoulder. Awww, shoot. I got a little worried and tried to break his concentration. I told him, "Man, you can't win!"

Outlaw was moving. Five minutes went by. Dig, lift, swing. Dig, lift, swing. Hup-ha! Outlaw chucked some snow my way! I brushed it off, laughing, "Ya still ain't gonna make it!"

Ten minutes! Outlaw was slowing down now. I looked over in the window and T.J. was loving it. Hell yeah, he'd get out faster so you know he was happy. He was just agrinning.

I told Outlaw, "That all you got, man?"

He started taking bigger scoops. I was begging the clock to hurry 'cause I didn't want Outlaw to beat me. It wasn't the money. Outlaw bragged too much already. I didn't need to hear about this the rest of my life. Naw sir! Bam! One minute left! Outlaw was doing good. I could tell he was getting close to a break. Thirty seconds! Now I was all excited because he's not going to make it. I start counting down like on TV, "Five . . . four . . . three . . . Time!"

Outlaw stopped, leaned on his shovel, and sweat was pouring off his ears. I'd gotten so excited that I was sweating too. I could feel sweat on my chest, making my long johns seem like they were squeezing my chest. I threw a clenched fist in the air! Outlaw rolled his eyes and finished the last of the digging. He was close. My man was close but hey, I had a clean tab! Outlaw took a hard stab at the snow and it broke away clean.

"Now it breaks," Outlaw said.

I gloated a bit 'til I got a smile out of him as he cleared the last of the snow away. Finally I said, "High five!"

I threw my right hand up and I swung my left hand out to pat Outlaw on his back. I got it up there and something grabbed it. I couldn't get my arm down. It froze in midair. Numb. Then this pain that I imagined lightning felt like hit my fingertips and shot all the way down to my corns. Sweet-Daisy-laid-out-like a-virgin-have-mercy-on-me! I ain't never felt a hurt like that. I didn't feel nothing but that pain. I looked down at my legs and they were just shaking. Shaking. I felt confused. What the hell was happening?

I thought I heard Outlaw say my name. And T.J. was in the window clawing the glass. I grabbed my chest and all the while I looked up at T.J. and I saw his lips moving and he was yelling. I didn't hear it, mind you. But I could read his lips. My boy was yelling my name. And then as I clutched my chest I felt Outlaw grabbing me around the shoulders and he ain't let my head hit the ground and I sho' appreciated that. I heard T.J. calling me but it wasn't in his man voice. Naw, I heard him in his child voice. That's some weird mess, huh? But that's what I heard. Then I saw T.J. standing over me and he ain't have on no coat. He just had on his designer sweater and slacks and I wanted to wave him away and say put your coat on, son, 'cause you catch cold so easy but I couldn't move my hands and I couldn't open my mouth.

T.J. dropped his eyes and had fear in his body. And when T.J. touched me, that's when I felt it. It went from him to me. I felt it when he hugged me to him and I couldn't hug him back. I'd had pain in the ring but I never lost touch. I was losing touch. I couldn't reach my boy, this pain was coming between us.

And then I heard a siren. Now, I did hear that. And my mouth got pasty and T.J. was clutching me so tight that I was getting hot and I felt the snow on the back of my legs; my pants legs were up, and I wanted to pull them down but I couldn't move. But more than that I wanted to reach my son and I couldn't. I was staring at him and all I saw was fear and I knew then. That's when it hit me. My heart was giving out and I was dying on my old front porch where I played marbles, and dominoes and kissing games. And Sweet Daisy have mercy, I was losing T.J., my son.

I closed my eyes and a thought came to me one word at a time just like my breath was coming one catch at a time. The thought was, Jesus. Is. My. Rock. In. Times. Of. Trouble. My mama used to say that. I'd ask her how she felt and she was ninety then and she never said, "Fine" or "Poorly." Mama would say, "Jesus is my rock in times of trouble." That was my thought. I wasn't ready to go. I wasn't ready to leave this earth. And I wasn't gonna lie because I had no great plans or great tasks left undone but I just wanted to live and appreciate the things I had. My son. My son I love and I always loved him and showed him love but look like it hit me as I lay there that I didn't appreciate the relationship. Maybe that was my downfall. Maybe that was why my heart was failing. I didn't appreciate things enough. My body had been good to me when I was young but I ain't appreciate that. I'd taken its strength for granted. I'd been drinking and smoking and partying and it was slipping away and I was about to lose out. Miss out. Miss out on all the good things.

And what would I do without T.J.? My son? We had more to do with each other. More times to share. He-he was gonna be a big-time musician, just was a matter of time, and I wanted to see that. I started hoping for that time. Hoping that time could be mine. And I wanted to talk to T.J. more, not about women and being a player like we always did, but about being a man and feeling and appreciating the people around you. I was looking at him and thinking about other folks I would be leaving behind and I just wasn't ready to go. It wasn't fair. Then I heard my own voice say, "Life deals the cards and you don't get a chance to cut." I'd told T.J. that. Now it was on me. But I wanted to stay here and I was scared that I was gonna get snatched away. I felt myself being moved. I closed my eyes and started to hear voices as someone started working on my chest. Jesus is my rock in times of trouble.

sandy

I'd gotten him back! At first I couldn't believe that I let Bebe talk me into doing it. But I had. And she was right! It felt good taking a knock at him. We'd gotten the stuff yesterday. That Liquid Nails is cheap. Two bucks a canister and the gun only cost four dollars. Bebe had a shovel she kept in her trunk in case she got stuck in one of those freak snowstorms we tend to get in Chicago. We took her car because T.J. knew mine. We didn't want to take a chance on him being up going to the bathroom or kitchen or something. If he got a glimpse of my car, he would get suspicious.

Anyway, we didn't go until like five in the morning. We didn't want anyone to see us. It was probably an unnecessary precaution because mostly old folks lived on T.J.'s block anyway. But why take a chance? Once we got the plan nailed down, it started working smoothly. I told Bebe I would do the back door while she started on the front. By the time I finished, I was able to come up and help her.

We were not playing! We wore commando outfits. All black. Black jeans. Black turtlenecks. Black coat. I was freezing too because the only black coat I owned was a leather bomber jacket and I tried to compensate with my thermoses but I still got cold piling up that snow. That was the hard part. Packing the snow. It took us about an hour to pile it up to where we were sure he wouldn't be able to get out quickly. I wanted him to miss that brunch. I wanted to mess with his mind. I wish I could have seen the look on his face when he opened the door! Bebe and I were sitting in the house laughing about it when the phone rang.

"That's him!" Bebe said.

I didn't even glance in the direction of the phone.

Bebe was like, "Answer it and tell him off!"

"Why? Let him stew!" I said.

Then I thought, I wanted to let him know I was home and that I meant it. So I picked up and told him, "Fuck you."

T.J. called right back and I told him again. Didn't he have nerve? T.J. knew he was wrong and he knew he had it coming. I didn't care if he was mad. Get mad. So what? I was mad. I was hurt. Let him see how it felt.

Now Bebe and I were still thawing out. We were drinking spiked hot cocoa and tea and we'd had turkey sausage and eggs and grits. I still had a chill in my bones, and my fingers were dirty red and they ached from shoveling and molding and squirting that glue. I was wondering how T.J. liked being trapped. How he liked being embarrassed. Wonder who he called to help him?

"The police," Bebe said.

That made me catch my breath and I said, "Can we get arrested?"

Bebe was like, "Girl, please, do you think the police are gonna waste their time on that?"

A laugh of relief came out of my mouth and I patted my chest. Bebe was right. The police wouldn't even deal with some mess like that on a serious level. The fire department?

Bebe laughed and said, "Yeah, they get cats out of trees, why not dogs out of houses?"

And we cracked up. Dogs out of houses! Yeah, I liked that analogy. I'd never gotten revenge on anyone before and I was surprised it felt as good as it did. It felt doggone good to me.

Bebe was like, "Let's drive by the house."

I said, "No way."

Bebe was bold. I was not that bold. But Bebe? She was. I said, "No."

But Bebe kept nagging and nagging and she said that T.J. didn't know her car and that we weren't going up in the driveway but just down the street a ways, just close enough to see how they were doing about getting him out of the house. Bebe swore we would turn around just as soon as we took a peek. And you know, I was starting to get convinced. I know that was silly. But she was making me curious and I felt like I'd gone this far, why not all the way? So we got in her car. Bebe started playing one of her tapes—Lakeside's *Fantastic Voyage*. Bebe could give you drama, okay? We were singing and driving and singing and driving. We felt cool and confident at first. Then the closer we got, the more nervous I became.

I said, "Naw, Bebe, let's turn around."

Bebe was trying to be cool but she was looking a little nervous too.

Bebe said something like, "Well, if you want to."

If I want to? She was going to put it off on me, which was perfectly fine. We were approaching T.J.'s block and I was like, "Be, don't turn down there, keep going." I looked down the street as we went past and I yelled, "Stop!"

There was an ambulance in T.J.'s driveway. The lights were flashing and stuff. And just as we stopped, the ambulance started taking off.

Bebe said, "What's going on?"

Like I knew. I said what she knew, "I don't know but something's wrong."

The ambulance took off with the siren going and Bebe started to follow it. She read my mind. We followed it all the way to the hospital. What could have happened? Before I knew it I started kneading my hands. Bebe was flying, laying on the horn trying to stay as close as she could to the ambulance without landing us inside one. I was trying to see what was going on inside the ambulance up ahead. But I couldn't really. I saw somebody's back and their hands working and that was just about it. We got to the hospital and I saw the paramedics jump out. They were wheeling Speed into emergency! T.J. ran behind them along with another older man. What happened? Bebe gunned her engine forward, then threw it into reverse and backed into a parking space. We got out and ran into the emergency room.

Bebe was saying, "Girl, I hope he's all right."

I said, "Me too!"

I know how I felt about my daddy and how scared I was when he had his stroke and died. I know how quick and scary it can be. We made it through the waiting area of the emergency room. There was a little girl sitting with her hand wrapped in a bloody towel. There was a teenaged boy with his leg in a cast and his girlfriend was with him. And there was an old couple sitting in the chair beneath a television set with a wobbly picture. He had his head in her lap and he was breathing and his wheezing was louder than the volume on the TV set. Then I saw the older guy who had gone in with T.J. and Speed. Bebe went to him as he talked on the phone.

I was walking toward T.J., and I said, "T.J., what happened?"

T.J. whirled around and it took a minute to focus on me, then he said angrily, "What-at are you doing here?"

I explained to him that Bebe and I went by the house and we saw the ambulance and we followed it here.

"Oh," he said sarcastically, "you just happened to go by? You all came by to see your handiwork?" He turned his back.

I got mad. "Yeah, we did but that's not important now—okay? That's all you ever think about is yourself—get over it, okay? What happened to Speed?"

T.J. took a deep breath, then shook his head and I could hear the anxiety in his voice rise. "I-I don't know, Sandy. One minute he was standing there cheering Outlaw on as he dug me out, and the next minute he was laid out. It just hit him out of nowhere."

Bebe came over with T.J.'s friend and he said, "Hi, I'm Out-law."

I was able to muster up a weak smile. "I've heard a lot about you and I just wish that we were meeting under better circumstances."

Bebe walked over and spoke to T.J. "I'm sorry to hear about your daddy."

T.J. kind of looked right through her, then nodded a thank-you. He just roamed off by himself.

Outlaw said, "Youngblood needs a little space."

T.J. stopped at the water fountain and gurgled a long sip of water. Then he came and sat down right in the middle of us, hung his head, and didn't say a word. It was as if he was there alone and deep in thought. The rest of us? Me, Outlaw, and Bebe just sat down around him. We sat down and waited.

bebe

Me and Sandy agreed to stay until we knew what was what. It was about an hour before the doctor came out. You know how they say time stands still? I know it's corny but I swear it did. That's what it felt like. Everybody stopped taking in air and just hoped and hung on to that hope like a valve on an air pump and not knowing whether it would turn or not.

The doctor said, "Mr. Willet will be fine. It wasn't a full-blown heart attack."

Everyone broke out in smiles and you could just feel the satisfaction and relief moving through the room. I took Sandy by the arm and said, "C'mon, the doctor said he'll be fine and we'll check back, but T.J. needs his space now."

And she knew I was right. Oh yeah, I was right.

t.j.

I have known fear. There was the horrible time when my mother died. I was afraid of the sound the ambulance made as it turned the corner. I was afraid of the silence and the stillness that covered her face as they rushed her to the hospital.

I have known fear. There was the time when I was in sixth grade eating one of those school baloney sandwiches and a piece got stuck in my throat and I couldn't breathe and the room started spinning and I fell backwards and hit my head and my mouth popped open and out popped a piece of baloney.

I have known fear. When I was sixteen in Daddy's new Deuce and a Quarter, me and a girl stopped at the lakefront at Thirty-first and pulled into a park up under the trees on a typical hot August night. It was humid everywhere else in the city except by the lake. The wind was skimming off the water and sailing through the window. I parked beneath the trees, faced the expressway, and doused the lights because it was after hours. The faint sounds of south Lake Shore Drive hummed as we watched a car or two go by in front of us.

I started to kiss my girl and it was starting to get awful good when suddenly a bright light was shining in our faces. A cop was standing there and told me to get out of the car. He was a big white guy with a red and black tattoo on his arm that said "Justice—Just Us." It was obviously on his skin and in his heart.

He grabbed me and threw me against the car and put his elbow in my back. I could feel his spit on the back of my neck. He told my girl to shut up because she had no business being out this late with a quote "punk" anyway. That cop pushed me around and even cuffed me to the door until he ran a check on the car. I was standing there looking like some kind of a criminal and I wasn't. I was just going home. My left leg was twitching and my throat was dry and I had a headache and I didn't know what that cop was going to do until he did it. He wrote me a ticket, uncuffed me, and told me and my girl to get our black asses going. I have known fear.

But never a fear this deep.

When I saw Daddy grab his chest like that and fall out on the porch. That was total fear. My own heart stopped. I watched him fall and it was like there was gas or something between us, not just air, because he fell slow and Outlaw ran slow and he caught his head before it hit the ground. I felt jealous because I wanted to do that. I wanted to catch him and hold him first. I pushed through the snow and I slipped. I knew my legs were wet and I had snow all in my shoes and I leaned over him. I know Daddy was in pain and it hurt. See, he had always tried to hide pain from me and I was glad his eyes were closed. I knew if our eyes met, he would try to hide the pain and I didn't want nothing that wasn't real between us.

I had a numbness in my gut and I felt like a helpless nothing and I had no control and no say-so and no power. And I wanted my daddy up and standing and talking shit and I had rarely seen him without that glaring cockiness he had. God, I like that. I envied that. And I saw him opening his eyes and I dropped mine because I didn't want him to see my fear and I hugged him close.

I heard Outlaw tell me the ambulance was on the way. And I eventually heard the siren but it took so long, it seemed. I heard it whining and the paramedics took over. I remember thinking, God, let me keep my daddy. I thought all of that on the way to the hospital and the paramedic guy tried to calm me by saying Daddy would be okay. But I felt helpless. I couldn't stop it, could

I? I couldn't protect him, could I? I couldn't heal him, could I? I didn't know that it was going to be okay and I felt cold, numb, and useless.

When we went into that emergency room, the first thing I noticed was the tame sound of a counterfeit rendition of "Feelings" playing. The second thing I noticed was the smell. It stunk! It smelled like bandages and damp steam heat. I looked at Daddy and he had his eyes open and he looked incredibly calm. He looked like he was waiting for a shave or something. No smile. But calm. Daddy was so cool. He was so fearless. The nurses stopped me at the door of the back room and me and Outlaw were told to go to the waiting room. He said he had to make a call. I just stood in the middle of the floor waiting. For what? I wanted my fear to leave. It was hurting me, holding me, and making me jumpy. I needed and wanted to calm down.

Then I heard Sandy's voice. All this fear I had seemed to turn into anger and I yelled at her and I'm ashamed to say that it felt good just to do something. Having anger and fear in your body at the same time is hell. She didn't take it, though. Sandy cooled me right out. I took a few steps and got a drink and tried to clear my head. I came back and I sat down and I just kept praying inside. I said the prayers Mama had taught me at my bedside. And at that moment I wished that I had been going to church.

I don't know how much time had passed but when the doctor did step out, it took my life away for what seemed like an eternity. Bam! Everybody froze. I heard the doctor say that Daddy was going to be all right and that brought me back to life. I felt weak, though. I was so relieved and the absence of fear left me nearly motionless. Sandy? We had locked horns but I knew we weren't through. I felt it. I knew everything was up in the air but I did manage a thank-you to them because they didn't have to stay. That was real nice that they did. Bebe took Sandy away.

Exhausted, I fell into a chair and Outlaw clasped my shoulder. And I put my head back and just relaxed. I was waxed and I told the nurse as she went by to let me know when I could talk to my father. I don't know how long I sat there. I dozed off for sure. What woke me was a soft kiss on the forehead. I opened my eyes and Miss Ann was there. I was so glad to see her. I hugged her and she said that Outlaw had called her and told her what happened. Outlaw had just left because he had to open the bar and she would stay with me. Miss Ann was sweet.

I explained to her what happened and she said, "Don't worry, Speed is as strong as a locomotive."

All I could think about was that I wanted to see my father.

Finally the doctor came out and said, "Your father would like to see you. He'll be fine but he's got to watch his diet and stop drinking. Talk to him but don't get him excited."

And the doctor patted my shoulder and walked me to the door. I was glad that he was walking me to the door because I don't know how long it would have taken on my own. What would I say? What would he say? I got closer and closer to the door and impulse took me over. I had a flood of emotion that I've never had before and I had a need, a desire, to do something.

I went in the room and Daddy was lying there. He looked weak but the thing I noticed most was that he looked very serious. Daddy-man always had a fun-loving kind of presence about him. It was stripped away now. He reached out and took my hand and he didn't take it like a shake, but like a hold. He reached out and held my hand. That's when I did it. I wanted to do it then because it felt right.

I said, "Daddy, I love you so much, man. I love you and I want you to know it because I thought I was losing you and I hadn't really said it clear, said it plain before now, and I just want you to know that. And I'm sorry and I just feel so bad about everything."

And I was trying to hold up but it was getting hard. I tried to will him to say something before I broke down because I didn't want to break down.

speed

T.J. had his mother's lips. I watched his lips as he talked to me. He told me he loved me. I knew. My boy showed me love with hugs and high fives, with the way he listened and imitated me. That's love. And I loved that boy so and that's why I had to do something, I needed to say something.

I said, "Son, I love you too. I damn near busted out of this life too soon."

T.J. looked real confused. I know he ain't know what I was jawing about but I was getting there. "Don't never rush nothing good," my pa used to say. "Don't rush nothing good." I had to go forward while I had the balls. I ain't never been afraid until now, so I had to deal with a few new things. I wanted to tell my son that he shouldn't live like me.

I said, "T.J., I've been living wild. I been living fast. Son, that's only good in doses and not for long stretches at a time and now my body is paying me back and it just ain't worth the bet that all the fun is worth that."

He looked more confused than ever.

I said, "I've been drinking and hanging out at lounges all my life and that's not a good thing. I been screwing and not loving damn near all my life with the exception of your mama. You standing in my dust and I'm trying to say it's not the place to be. Now, don't get me wrong, son, I'm not saying go sit down somewhere and be a boring, miserable nobody. Live. I want you to live. It's in you to live like it's in me but I'm saying don't go buck-wild like me—measure. There are important relationships in your life and if you're out fucking around all the time you'll never get the best out of them. I don't want you to miss out. I don't want you to run into bad health like me. I want you to know what's up. 'Cause I'm fixin' to do some changing and it won't be drastic but it'll be substantial. Yes sir! Don't trip out on me, son, 'cause I ain't had no big religious experience or nothing but I just had the shit scared out of me because I almost went too soon by my own doing and I realized that I love you and want to be around you more than anything else in the world."

T.J. was starting to understand, I think. At least that dumbfounded look was off his face. A nurse came in and said that Ann was outside and that made me smile.

T.J. said, "You want to see her?"

I nodded yes and I told T.J. to stay. I was going to come clean all the way. I was going to make a new start, so if you're gonna be fresh be fresh. I saw Ann and I felt warm inside. She had on a jogging suit, royal blue. Her hair was tousled and she looked a little worried but I could tell she was trying to play it off.

Ann said, "Negro, what is your problem scaring everybody?"

I liked me some Ann. I wasn't in love with her and I knew it was because I never gave it a chance. It was just sex. T.J. thought Ann and I had always been friends but he didn't know what I was about to tell him now.

I said, "T.J., I want to tell you something and I want you to understand it like I'm telling you now. Your mother was a wonderful woman. When she was healthy, wasn't nothing that could compare to Shine."

T.J. said, "I know, Daddy."

And I had to tell him, "Shut up and listen now."

He got quiet then. I was feeling like my old self but I was getting tired, so I wanted to hurry.

I looked at Ann and I continued. I said, "When your mother got sick, she became like a child to me. She was someone who I

215

had to protect, and to take care of, not someone who could give me the companionship that a husband needs from a wife. But Shine was sick, understand? I got her the best of everything and I know you know that. But you have to understand what I'm saying and how everything was."

Ann mumbled something about having to go.

And I said, "Where you going? Don't run!?" She'd been after me for years to tell T.J. and now she wanted to run.

I said, "T.J., I needed a woman to satisfy my needs, for companionship, while I was still married to your mama and that person was Ann."

T.J. got this weird blank look on his face. I expected him to say something. So I kept going. I made it plain. I said, "Man, I wasn't in love with Ann and Ann wasn't in love with me. I didn't see the harm in it because I had needs. A man has needs. But now I see how I could have done better. How I could have waited and when I did kick it with Ann here, how I could have made something more out of it. But I was so buck-wild that I pissed it away. I'm saying to you don't piss folks away. Now y'all go'n 'cause I'm tired. Go on now and get the hell out. Hear? I'm tired. And I'm through."

t.j.

All this time he'd been lying to me. My daddy, who I thought never would lie to me about something important, had lied to me. Now, Daddy would say he was trying to protect me or that it wasn't any of my business no way. But Daddy had gotten scared, scared about dying, and he told it.

I stumbled out of there dazed. I don't even know what Miss Ann said to me. I heard her mumbling something softly but I kept going. I wasn't mad at her. How could I be? Daddy was smooth, especially back then, and I know if she was what he wanted he wasn't going to stop 'til he got her. Period. Case closed. So I wasn't blaming Miss Ann. I just had to get some air because this was too much.

He'd been telling me all this time that it was okay to be a player, that a dude should be a player because one day you'll find that right person and that's who you can build a life with. Mama was supposed to be that person. He said she was. Daddy had set her apart in my mind, had put her in her own special place. Now he told me something different. Which Daddy was I supposed to believe? Player Speed. Scared Speed. I'm not a child. I'm not being childish in my ways either. I'm just being real. Someone tells you something long enough you believe it's real. Now his logic, his teachings, were counterfeit. So what, I'm grown, right? The so part is, I only have the foundation that he gave me and now he had smashed it. I wasn't sure I wanted the new foundation Daddy was turning over.

Could I ever believe him again? He was saying don't do as I do, but do as I say. That old bullshit. Who wants to get into that? He played on my mama when she was down and sick. Daddy-man! C'mon! I know you like to get all the leg you can. I know it. You told me that. Get it. Get it. Gone. But it was supposed to be different with Mama. Does that mean that no one will ever be able to capture my loyalty? Does it mean I don't have to give it as long as I take care of the person, love the person, and don't put it in her face it's okay to do whatever I want? Are those the rules? What are the rules now? Ain't none. Were there ever any?

Now I'm in the game and I'm confused what to do. And I'm mad. And what a cop-out. He dropped the bomb, then said, "Get out." What? I couldn't question him. I couldn't go off on him like I want because he's sick. And I have never, ever gone off on Daddy. I never wanted to. Never needed to. But now I'm mad! What a chicken! He tells me when I'm feeling sorry for him. I'm feeling sorry that he's got a begging heart. I'm mad and I want to scream and shout and slam the walls but I want him to see it. I want him to hear it. I want Daddy to know. But I can't!

Man, Daddy-man just up and stole on me. Daddy snuck up on me and stole on me, pa-dow! Right in the heart! Know what I'm saying? I've got to tell myself to stop taking this so tough. But I can't. I can't get it out of my mind. I'm not going to the hospital. I don't want to make a mistake and say or do something that might upset him. I'm just going to call. Doc said that he's fine and will be out in a couple of days and that's cool.

What am I going to say? I can't pretend that nothing happened. I can't question him and get him excited. And I know it will show all over my face. And Daddy will ask, want to dig around and pull something out, and then what? I don't want to fight with him. This is raw enough, what do I need more for?

And Sandy? Why did she do some wild crap like that? How could she not know I didn't care about Tia at all? Man! And for her to plot like that against me. Tia? That thing wasn't planned—it happened and was meaningless. It was a little skin slapping and nothing more. But Sandy sat down and schemed on me! She wanted me to miss that brunch and she knew how important it was to me. Now, what's up with that? What's going to happen to us now? I don't even know what I want. I don't know what she wants. I don't even want to deal with it. I don't want to deal with her. This—this . . . uh . . . all this at one time is too much. I need to get my thoughts together, and until then I can't see Sandy or Daddy.

fifty-seven

sandy

I called T.J. that night and the next day and he would not talk to me. I couldn't say that I totally knew how he felt but I had a firm handle on the fear he had about almost losing his father. My daddy had died from a stroke.

I was in my junior year of college and I was home for spring break. I had just gone to a Kappa mixer with three of my girls who had stayed in the city to go to school. We all wore black minis and thought, knew, and actually were, looking good. It would have been 100 percent fun except for that Kappa punch. Grain alcohol. Fruit punch. Vodka. Gin. Limes. And with all that stuff in it, don't you know it was smooth? I had one glass before I knew it was spiked and had enough sense to stay away. But I still got a dull headache about a half an hour later. My girls drank three or four cups apiece. I turned out to be the designated driver and it took a while to get everybody home and we were so happy. We'd each pulled a good-looking guy at the party and were talking about going to the movies together on Sunday and we felt good because we were having fun and we were young and smart and could have the world.

When I got home, there was a note on the door from Mama that said to go to Christ Hospital. That was it. I ran next door and my neighbor drove me because I was afraid to drive by myself. In the car my heart just ached because I knew it was Daddy. He had super-high blood pressure. High blood pressure was the number one killer of black people.

I sat in that car and hoped and prayed for him and I wanted to

220

know why. Why did someone who worked that hard have to suffer? I was afraid. I was tight all over. I was so stiff I could hardly get in the car. My legs didn't want to lift. My arms didn't want to fold. But I had to get in that car. What if I lost him? What would I do? Just the thought ate a hole in my gut and I rested my head forward in my palms and it only served to slide the ache in a new direction. I felt angry at myself. I remember feeling I had everything. I had my health. My youth. My entire life was ahead of me. What would I do if I lost him? He and Mama were so important to me! They each played a part and gave me parts of what I was, what I wanted, and what I hoped to be. And with a part missing how could I survive? Wouldn't I crumble? Wouldn't I grieve away into dust?

That is the kind of stuff I'm sure T.J. had to be feeling. He had to be scared to death. Could he deal with it? He always wanted to be Irish Spring—manly man. That was a commercial, not real life! Daddy survived that stroke but would die from another two years later but my mind and my heart started to prepare after that first scare. That first lick is the hardest to take. The death of T.J.'s mother was hard for him, sure, but as a child your mind has less to pick over. You know less, so you worry less, I would imagine. T.J.'s father has always been a huge part of his world, so this kind of scare, this lick, would rip him to the core.

Now I wondered, would he mend? Or would he be a nervous wreck always pampering, worrying about, his father? I decided to go visit Speed that third day. I wanted to see how he was doing. I remember when my father was in the hospital that it always cheered him up to have visitors. I stood outside the door for a long time before pushing it open. I'm not sure what I was waiting on. A shot of courage maybe? Maybe. I figured Speed would call me on my little igloo stunt, but hey, I would just have to deal with it.

Speed's room was blooming with color from bright flowers and get-well cards. But Speed himself? He was lying there, pale, but he didn't look bad at all, just a bit weak and he was quiet. I didn't know him that well, but from what T.J. had told me and from the dinner, I knew quiet was not his regular thing. He looked disturbed. Troubled. I'm sure he was worried about being sick. That made me extra glad I'd decided to visit. I could take his mind off his weak heart if only for a little while.

I said, "Excuse me."

And he turned and looked at me and just for a second there was something in his eyes and I thought, He's going to let me have it for trapping T.J. in the house.

Speed said, "Well, if it ain't the queen of the Ice Capades!"

And it was friendly. I felt a big block of air leave me and I was so relieved.

I went over to him and said, "Can I give you a kiss?"

And Speed winked and said, "Never have in my life turned down a kiss from a lovely lady."

And I gave him one on the cheek. I told him T.J. just made me mad and I wasn't trying to hurt him, just wanted to get him back. Speed listened and nodded and then he said that he knew I wasn't trying to hurt T.J. and that it was nothing hateful.

Speed said, "You ain't try and hurt my boy! Shoot, girl, I've known women that have tried to cut folks and whatnot, so I know you ain't try to do nothing dirt wrong." Then he gave a serious smile. "But don't do no shit like that again, hear?"

And I laughed and nodded okay. No more plots or commando runs for me. We talked a little more about him getting out the next day and neither one of us brought up T.J. I thought he would. Speed must of thought I would. It was awkward. Neither of us did. I was dying to ask about T.J. but if Speed didn't say anything, I know T.J. must of told him that he wasn't talking to me and probably Speed wanted to stay out of it.

After I left the hospital I went over to the job. I'd been off a couple of days and I called ahead and asked Harvey for a meeting. I went straight to his office. Harvey had an open-door policy and that was cool. I asked his secretary, Diana, if I could go in and she said he had someone else in and that it would be about a half-hour wait. Doggone it! I didn't want to wait. Diana was making a Starbucks run and offered to pick me up a coffee too but I said no thanks. I just sat in the chair and picked up *Broadcasting* magazine and glanced through. I thought about what I wanted to say. I wanted to say, "Thank you, Harvey, for your confidence and the work that you've given me here but I've decided that I would like to pursue other avenues." Harvey would argue with me. He would try to convince me to stay. But I really didn't want to have to deal with Tia and the petty work gossip. I'd called and found out that only the position at the all-news radio station was still open. The format wasn't to my liking but the job paid more. I could have it if I wanted it. A lot of people move around like crazy in this business. It's odd for someone to stay a long time in one place. That's what I told myself.

Anyway, I was sitting there waiting, nervous, but determined to give my two weeks' notice and I felt someone lean over me and whisper, "Can I see you in the rest room?" I looked up at Tia and I could have slapped her. I mean it took all my self-control not to haul off and smack her.

Tia whispered, "Please?"

And I followed her to the ladies' room. I let her go first. I didn't want a snake like her walking behind me. As soon as we got inside Tia demanded, not asked, demanded to know what I was waiting to see Harvey about. I told her that it was none of her business.

Tia was very firm and threatening when she said, "Well, if you blab about me erasing your files, I'll say you lied and tell him all about Mr. T.J.!"

I wanted to deck her and I'm not a violent person. I said,

"Don't threaten me because I'm nobody's pushover. I was going to quit and just leave it all alone but you have pushed me too far."

She thought she was bad? Who?!

I told her, "You think you're bad but, girlfriend, I'm about to run you in the ground. I can outsell you and outwork you with a migraine and crutches. I'm not holding back anymore. I don't have to fight dirty like you—erasing files and whatnot—no, I'm going to blitz you because I'm sharper and just better in every way."

Tia responded, "Stupid bitch!" and gave me the finger.

I told her, "And you'll be seeing this stupid bitch every day looking fine at eight A.M. ready to show your trifling butt up!"

Tia left and I just looked in the mirror and I felt good. Do you hear? Bebe would be proud of me and it didn't matter if she was or wasn't because I was proud of myself.

I left the bathroom and checked Harvey's office. Diana wasn't back and Harvey's door was closed. I went back out into the hallway and I ran into Jackson, who'd worked on the graphics for the project. He had on a bad blue Armani cardigan sweater that matched his eyes. He gave me a hug and his pudgy belly rubbed coochie-coo against my ribs.

Jackson said, "Bonus time coming! Like the sweater I charged until our bonus checks come through?"

Then Jackson told me about how well the presentation went and he said that Tia did a good job but not as good as I would have done. I appreciated that. Jackson was cool. I wondered if he'd heard the gossip. Could his mind be kicking it around behind that praise and warm smile?

My next thought led me to the cafeteria. Since I decided to stay, I might as well face the folks. A narrow walkway leads to a big room with a bunch of vending machines—chips, pop, ice cream, hot coffee—and people hang around there to gossip. Just like I thought, there were three people from sales there among the crowd. I went right to their group. I wanted to get it over with. I was cleaning house today.

I walked up and said, "Hi."

Everybody said hello back nice-nice.

And I just said, "I know there's been some gossip from Tia about her and the man I'm seeing."

Nobody said a word—they all just looked. You'da thought I pulled out a gun on them or something. But from the look in their eyes, yeah, she'd talked. Tia had definitely been flapping those sausage lips.

So I said, "All that talk is B.S. and I don't want that to interfere with what I have to do here. If Tia wants to do that, then that is her low-class business but I just want to let you all know once and for all there's no wool being pulled over my eyes and I'm here to get paid, how about y'all?"

One of the ladies smiled and the other two looked agreeable. Didn't I just give them something to talk about and at the same time shut them up too?

Then I went back to Harvey's office. When I came in, Diana was coming out of the office. She gave me a big smile and sipped on her coffee. She said Harvey was ready to see me now. I went right in.

Harvey was sitting at his big oak desk and said, "How are you feeling?"

I told him better, remembering I said I had the flu, and then I sat down in the chair closest to him.

Harvey asked, "What did you want to see me about?"

Now I was going to lie and say that I wanted to thank him for the opportunity of working on the project and I just wanted to know how it went. But Harvey had always been up front with me. And I had friends at other places and they naturally cried the blues about their bosses. Here I had a gem, so I laid out the truth.

I said, "Well, I was coming in to quit." Harvey didn't look surprised at all. What was up with that? I wondered.

He asked, "Aren't you happy here?"

I told him I was very happy here but that I had gotten a better offer and I was going to take it for personal reasons but I changed my mind and decided to stay.

Harvey broke out in a big smile and said, "I'm glad you didn't lie to me, Sandy."

What was he talking about? Harvey went on and said that Diana had stopped in the ladies' room on her way out and she heard my conversation with Tia! Diana had run right back and told Harvey all about it. Harvey said that at the end of the day he was going to fire Tia. I wanted to jump for joy. She was going to get hers! I played it cool and didn't say anything. Harvey said that he didn't need anyone working for him that would use sabotage to get ahead. Thank you, Jesus! Yeah-yeah! I cheered like crazy on the inside and played it cool on the outside. I told Harvey thanks for having confidence in me and the foresight to correct the situation with Tia since I felt uncomfortable about being directly responsible for someone else losing their job. Was I on a roll or what? Harvey gave me the rest of the week off. Then I got this worry: what would everybody say? Would they say I got Tia fired because of T.J.?

Harvey must of got wind of what I was thinking. He said, "I'm going to post a memo about Tia and the exact reason she's being fired and I think it will make things around here quite comfortable and clear for everyone."

Was I on a roll or what? When I left Harvey's office, I stopped and bought a lottery ticket.

I went home and I was feeling great. I felt a big burden had been lifted off me. I was booting around my apartment, cleaning up, playing some Whitney Houston, and I hopped in the shower. I wasn't going to call T.J. I was going to go to the club where he worked. I was going to make this boy talk to me. We were going to have it out one way or another. I knew he was still playing at the same place. He told me the gig ended on the seventh. And it was only the fifth and . . . The fifth? I got a chill to beat all chills. I ran into my bedroom and got my date book and looked.

fifty-eight

bebe

I had my feet soaking in some warm water and Epsom salts. I was feeling fabulous. I was comfortable and decided to watch a little tube. I flicked on the television and what did I see? NASA sending up a shuttle. Why do we keep shooting shuttles up in space? What's up there? Every time you turn around NASA is blasting off a shuttle! They're just nuking money, okay? Are there homeless people up there? Hungry babies? A cure for cancer or AIDS? I'll answer my own question, no! Well, blast off some dollars down here where it counts! Lift off the burden of some of the people who live right here on earth. Bump all the petri dishes and astro veggies growing in space. Bump bringing back those Kodak moments of the stars. Picture this instead: some hungry kids eating a decent meal, less expensive medicine for the old folks, and cut a big plug why don'tcha out of my taxes. I ought to run for Congress!

The phone rang and it was Sandy.

"Beeeee-Be," she said.

I smiled and said, "San-daaaay!"

She said, "Girl, call a doctor."

I said, "What's wrong?"

And then I got ready to go into the blackberry thing but Sandy said, "I think I'm pregnant."

Whoa! That's not how the game is supposed to go. I said, "For real?"

Sandy moaned the affirmative. I heard a drumroll in my head when I asked her how late she was. Sandy said she was four days late. Four days?

228

Sandy was like, "Yeah, four days."

"When did you notice?"

"I've been so worked up over Tia and T.J., his daddy, and all the stuff at work and my meeting with Harvey that I totally forgot about it until just now."

Now I was thinking fast, hoping to get her mind off of it. I said, "How'd it go with Harvey?"

Sandy perked up a little and gave me a condensed story about how Tia tried to front her in the bathroom. That Tia was stank! She had nerve and a half, didn't she? I was so proud of Sandy when she told me she had cut her off at the knees that I didn't know what to do. I said, "Yeah, get her treacherous behind!"

Then Sandy said, "She got busted because Harvey's secretary was in the bathroom and we didn't know it. She heard the whole thing!"

Now Sandy was staying and Harvey was giving Tia the boot. God is good, isn't he? Then there was this long pause.

Sandy said, "I was on a roll."

"You still on a roll," I said. "Lots of folks come late."

"Yeah but my aunt from Red Bank is usually timely, nothing past a day or two."

"First time for everything," I said. "Plus haven't you been under a heap of stress these last few weeks?"

Stress can throw your cycle off too now. I asked her if she had a kit at home and Sandy didn't. She was about to start worrying, I could feel it. She was already nervous-sounding.

Sandy said, "My palms are sweating."

I said, "Calm down."

She had options. One—she could wait a couple of more days and then truly freak. Two—she could go out and buy a kit and give herself the test at home. Three—she could get the kit, come over to my place, and take the test so she didn't have to wait by herself.

"Which one?" I asked.

Sandy said, "I can't wait, Be, I can't stand it. No way!"

Then I X'd the right choice and said, "Girl, just come over here and we'll see what's up."

"But suppose I am?" Sandy whined.

"Well, don't trip before you have to because you'll just be wasting all that energy and emotion for nothing and you'll be all drained and tired for nothing," I told her.

"But suppose I am?" Sandy said again.

"You're not," I said.

If she had been six months showing, I would have lied and said she wasn't pregnant, okay? I could feel Sandy winding up. When she got wound up, Sandy was hard to calm down. That child could drive you crazy. She could worry the frost off an ice cube, okay? Sandy, think positive. That's what I told her.

Then she said, "Be, I'm coming."

I said, "Okay."

fifty-nine

sandy

It's not like I haven't had this happen before—I've been late before. One or two days, but four? I don't know what to do with my hands except wrap them around myself and wonder. I'm still standing still, not moving, maybe I can feel my body working. Maybe I can sense what's going on inside. Like an itch, maybe I can feel and locate a tinge of presence. Something. Anything. Presence. Presence of what? The end of a cycle, the beginning trickle of relief or would it be life? I don't need this. A baby? What a responsibility and what a burden. A baby is for people like Mama. People who have instincts, who have time, and who know what to do. Humpf, I just thought of something funny. I remember my sophomore year of high school my girlfriend Rhonda thought she was pregnant. She said her cousin told her if you drank three cans of tomato juice and stood on your head for a half an hour your period would come. I can't help but laugh, but you know if I thought it might work, I'd be a red-lipped upside-down fool praying for a miracle right now!

I've got to know because worrying is a major part of my nature. So let me just get myself together and go on over to Bebe's place. I rushed around and put on some heavier clothes, grabbed my coat, and headed out the door. There's a grocery slash drugstore in the lower back half of the building. I went in, bought the kit, and walked back through the lobby. I put my hand on the revolving door and whose face meets mine? T.J.'s! My luck was absolutely running out.

t.j.

Sandy looked startled to see me. I know she was surprised. How could she know I was coming? She had no way of knowing. I hadn't returned any of her calls. Nothing. I didn't know myself what I was going to do until I did it. I jetted over hoping to catch her and I didn't call first in case I changed my mind. I was just lucky enough to catch her as she was going out. We needed to talk. Sandy just nodded and clutched the little brown bag she had and then stuck it under her arm.

I asked her, "What you got—cookies?"

Sandy didn't say a word. That silence can be a killer. All the way up in the elevator she stared at the little lights flashing on the panel. Like she was counting? We knew what floor we were going to. Then she turned and looked at me. Her eyes. Those expressive, bigmouth eyes? They did some talking. They said, I'm pissed off at you, man. I'm hurt and I'm afraid. And those eyes said, What do you want from me? What's up with us? That's what those eyes were saying to me. I wanted to close them with a swipe of the hand.

Did I have answers? Absolutely not. I was mixed-up and unsure and why stay dragging around not knowing what the deal was? I was still kind of mad about what she did. Who told her to build an igloo outside my door? Hey, that was some psycho stuff. Maybe one day she would get pissed at me and cut up my clothes or something. Sandy showed me a side I didn't think was there. But I knew I wasn't afraid of her or anything foolish like that. But I needed to see her, talk to her, to decide what we were going to do about us. All I could feel was tension. Isn't that something? Thick tension was all I felt in that elevator. We got off and went into her apartment. I slipped off my coat and sat on the couch.

Sandy asked, "You want a drink?"

"Yeah," I said, "we both need one, I think."

She looked real funny at me. I wasn't trying to make her nervous. I wasn't. I was just talking. I did need a drink. She for damn sure looked like she needed one.

Sandy handed me my glass and she said, "I saw your father today."

She went to see Daddy? I had checked on him by phone but I hadn't been there. I wasn't ready to deal with that right now. One thing at a time. I wondered briefly if he had mentioned our problem to her but I realized quickly that he wouldn't do that.

I said real cool, "What did Daddy say?"

And Sandy said that he said he was feeling very good and that he was glad to be getting out of the hospital tomorrow.

I nodded and said, "Sandy, sit down."

And she did sit but at the other end of the couch.

"Move over," I told her, and patted the pillow next to me.

She did.

I was starting to get irritated. She needed to drop this aloof crap.

"C'mon," I said, "we're adults and need to talk."

Sandy finally spoke and proved she did have a voice. "You go first."

Now, I didn't come there with a plan or a speech because I didn't know what I wanted to do. I wasn't exactly sure how I was feeling about us.

I said, "Sandy, this is hard for me because I don't know what I'm feeling. I'm over that ice cube crap and I'm sorry Tia busted your chops and she was wrong to tell you 'cause it wasn't really anything to it. She knew that, period. It was just sex."

Sandy said, "Sex? Is that all you thought about? T.J., I thought we were special to each other. I thought we could build something special together, a long-term relationship with each other. All you had on your mind was sex! You're just looking to get some! Not only did you show your behind, T.J., you showed your dog collar too!"

That pissed me off. I felt a vein pop out on the side of my neck.

I told Sandy, "That's the problem with women, you fantasize too much! You don't let a brother shake the snow off his shoes before you're sizing him up for a tux and a ring. What's up with that? From the word Hi, a woman is calculating how soon she can walk down that aisle, about leaving that phony girlfriend out of the wedding party, thinking about who the kids will look like and all that. One date and a woman's on the phone burning up the wire, 'Oh, girlfriend, this could be it! Girl, he could be the one!' C'mon? After one date! But that's y'all's M.O.! Fantasy! Fantasy!"

Sandy said, "Stop exaggerating!"

"I'm not—this is truth. A man is straight with a woman. He goes in for what it is. We don't go in with expectations. We see a new relationship possibly, a way to have fun definitely. A dude wants to enjoy the woman, he's not looking long-range. He's focused on what's before him then. Not next month. Next year. He's not thinking about will she be a good wife, if she can cook, or about babies and all that! For what? That's a female thing. That's what derails relationships most of the time. Women don't see Doug, Steve, or Tommy. They see Mr. Husband and start building expectations from there. Women are looking one way and men, we're looking another way."

sandy

"And we can't see each other! Women are not the entire problem, T.J. Men are tripping too! Sure, women are always hoping to meet someone special. What's wrong with that? What's wrong with hoping to build something good, strong, and special?"

"Nothing," T.J. said, "if women wouldn't go off the deep end from the start!"

"T.J., everyone hopes for good things in life, so just leave that alone. And you're right, men are for the moment but not like you describe! You see, from the time a man helps you off with your coat, if he helps you off with your coat, he's trying to figure out how to get the rest of your clothes off. Men are too physical. Men pick women on how they look. They're thinking sex! Women don't judge on looks alone and aren't preoccupied with sex. Sure we'd like a handsome, sexy guy—why not? But we do our choosing on how a man talks to us, the way he treats us initially. Men start off talking sweet to us, talking to us as if they are truly interested in our feelings.

"Men will show you sensitivity for a minute to draw you in. But once they figure we're hooked and they are used to our beauty and our bodies, they start to get funky. Yes you do! Is that fair? Be more sensitive to our needs and wants. Anyone wants a person to talk to them in a real manner and they want to be listened to in return. I know you guys got it in you but why do we have to try and search and drag it out? Come to the table correct. You're right about one thing, T.J. Men are looking one way and women are looking another and we can't seem to hook up. When will the lines of communication open?"

235

T.J. said, "We're talking. I'm trying to tell you what the deal was. Me and Tia just had a sex thing. It didn't mean anything."

"So what?" I said. "T.J., how do you think that makes me feel that you took some sex just because it was out there to be had? You just had to have some tits and ass and with somebody that was going to put it all in my face later? What's that about?"

I knew what it was about. It was about his player role. His masculine role. His I'm-a-young-stud role.

"Tia told everyone in the office and embarrassed the heck out of me! I'd been bragging about your black ass and Tia had them laughing behind my back! How would you feel?" I asked him. "How would you feel?"

t.j.

She was sweating now and shouting. Sandy acted like I had sought Tia out. I hadn't.

I told Sandy, "Hey, she came to me. I didn't seek her out—she chased me down."

"Was that the first or the second time or what time was it?" Sandy said with the nastiest look I'd ever seen on her face.

I found myself explaining, "The first time we kicked it you and I weren't even hanging out together yet. The second time you blew me off, remember?"

If she had left her job and come to the club like we planned, then Tia never would have gotten in. That's how she got in. Sandy wasn't taking care of personal business! And I told Sandy that and she waved me off like I was some kind of a chump.

"Please," she said, "you don't have any more gumption than to think that Tia was dying for you that much? She was trying to get to me was all. She was using you to play games with me and the job, trying to move me out of the way at the top. Can't you see that?"

No, I couldn't see that. Tia wasn't using me. She just likes to kick it is all. She wanted some of me and I, at the time, was mad at Sandy, and wanted her. It was lust. Sandy was dipping into this conspiracy theory.

"This ain't Whitewater," I told her. "It was sex and nothing more!"

Hadn't she lusted after someone before with no intent of it going further than the sheets?

I asked her, "Haven't you had sex with somebody before and wanted nothing more than that?"

Sandy said, "No."

What a big lie!

sandy

So what, I lied. I said no because I didn't want him to know that. He wanted justification and I wasn't going to give it. No way. One-night stands? Hey, I had only one in my entire life although I had met some guys who I wanted real bad just for then. But I have self-control and most of all I don't want to make sex cheap. To me, some over-the-counter feel-good thing that's easy to get. What's the point? Add to that all the diseases out there too? All the consequences? I use protection whenever I make love. I have a diaphragm and my partners have condoms. But I was still late, wasn't I? I was here arguing with him. And I could be pregnant with his child and he could be the father of mine and he was talking about OPP? I cared about T.J. I cared about this boy, and his touch, his looks, had said that he cared about me, but now I wasn't sure.

I told him, "You act so selfish sometimes."

"How?" he shouted. "How am I selfish?"

I laid it out. I talked about all the ways I had cared for him and helped him.

He said, "Don't throw that in my face."

Now, he asked and I was throwing it in his face? I was talking to him. I was telling T.J. how I felt. I wasn't badgering him. I wasn't trying to diss him. I had feelings!

T.J. said, "I know you do and I respect that or I wouldn't be here talking to you."

He was saying one thing but I couldn't put it together with his actions. God, this was getting messier and messier. Then the phone rang.

I leaned over to answer it and T.J. frowned. "Don't even think about it."

I gave T.J. my very best fuck-you look. This was my house, wasn't it? I answered the phone and it was Bebe. I said, "Hi, Be."

T.J. rolled his eyes and mouthed the words Bye-bye.

Bebe started asking me questions and I gave one-word answers, "No. No. Yes. Yes. I don't know. No. Yes."

Then T.J. snatched the phone out of my hand and hung it up.

bebe

Sandy said she was coming right over, so when it had been a while I called to see what the holdup was. She answered the phone and I said, "You haven't left yet?"

And Sandy said, "No."

Then I asked her if she was okay and she said, "No."

"Is T.J. there with you?" I asked.

She said, "Yes."

"Y'all fighting?" I asked.

She said, "Yes."

"Are you going to tell him that you think you might be pregnant?" I asked.

Sandy said, "I don't know."

"Want to know what I think?" I started.

But Sandy said, "No."

"Are you okay?" I asked.

Sandy said, "Yes."

Then T.J. grabbed the phone and said, "She's busy."

Then he hung up on me. It took all my strength not to call back or go over there and tell that Negro off. Telling me to shut up is what he was doing. Mr. T.J. was just taking over everythang. I know he was over there sweating my girl. My heart went out to her. But I was cool. Maybe I did need to stay out of Sandy's business. I just sat down and hoped for the best for her. But God, I was dying to know what was going on!

sixty-five

sandy

"What is your problem?" I asked T.J.

He said, "I'm tired of Bebe being in our business. Bebe is nosy and needs a man to keep her busy so she can mind her own damn business."

I told him, "For your information she called because I was on my way over there when I got stopped in the lobby, so she was just checking to see what happened."

T.J. backed off a little but not much.

I let him have it. "Don't you ever snatch a phone I pay for out of my hand. I pay the bills here, T.J." And then I got real evil and it wasn't like me but I said, "And as I recall I've paid a few bills over at your place too."

Bang! That got him right in the ego. T.J. got mad and as red as hot coals.

"Uh-huh, you don't have to do shit for me, Miss Atkins," he said. "Don't throw up in my face the things you did for me. You did what you wanted to do. I didn't have on a mask or a gun, so don't go there. You offered, and I accepted, what was I going to say, no? I wasn't trying to bleed you, honest to God I wasn't, and you know it. We were kicking it and having fun together. Men and women should have fun together, enjoy each other to the utmost. That's the kind of brother I am. Now, as for the money and stuff? I thought you truly wanted to help me, so I accepted it for what it was, help. Understand?"

No. T.J. was apparently looking for an apology and when I didn't give it he really got pissed off.

T.J. jumped up and went to the door and said, "Tell you what—you don't have to worry about doing *nothing* for me anymore, okay?"

He grabbed his coat off the chair. It was under mine and my bag fell onto the floor. Out popped the kit. T.J. just stared at it.

I said, "I might be pregnant."

Why did I blurt it out like that? Because I was scared. I was worried. Why not him? He put me in mind of that kid game, Statue. He froze. I don't even think his eyes moved.

t.j.

Pregnant? The word fell off a cliff inside my brain.

I looked up at her and said, "Do you know for sure?"

Sandy let out what sounded like something between a sigh and a yawn and slid down on the couch. She shook her head no, then bit the tip of her thumbnail. I saw a piece of hazel polish chip away and it stuck to the soft part of her lower lip.

"I'm four days late," she said.

I picked up the kit and said, "You were going over to Bebe's to take the test?"

She nodded yes.

I asked her, "So when were you going to call me?"

"As soon as I was positive," Sandy said, "I was going to call."

I felt like she was blowing up the room. We were fighting and now this? A child? I didn't want a child. I wasn't ready for children. Children want and need so much from you and when you fall short it hurts too bad. Just the thought of being a father made me think of Daddy. I'd be standing in his shoes. Would I want my son to be as harsh as I was being against him? Could I take the scrutiny that I was putting on my old man? The tables would be turned and could I measure up now? I didn't know. I didn't feel confident. Sandy thought she read my face.

She said, "Don't say it."

No! She was trying to control everything and I was tired of it!

I said, "Damnit, you listen to me. Let me have a say, I have a right to have a say. I want you to take the test now, here with me. If you're pregnant I will be the father and it's going to be my responsibility. You don't have to run off and hide under a friend's wing."

Sandy looked at me and I saw that she felt some relief and she slowly got up.

sandy

I walked over to him and took the kit out of his hand.

I said, "I'll go in and take the test and we can wait together."

T.J. nodded. He looked awful scared. It was clear that neither one of us wanted a baby. But if forced, could he handle the responsibility? T.J. didn't say, but he was trying very hard to be responsible now. I reached and touched his hand as I walked past him and headed to the bathroom. I touched him but he didn't touch me back. I looked up and stared at him. His eyes were determined yet blank. I couldn't get a read on what was going on behind that glazed look. I went in and shut the door.

The hair on my arms was standing up and I dashed cold water in my face. Taking the test was no big deal. Very quick. I brought the little plastic container back and set it on the table. We would wait for the signal . . . red for yes, a blue for no. He sat there and just stared at it. I stared at it too.

I set it in the middle of the table and finally I said, "If it's yes? What do you want to do?"

T.J. said, "Let's wait."

No, I didn't want to wait. I wanted to know how he felt, right now under pressure. I didn't want a child, was not ready for one.

I asked him again, and I brought his face toward mine with both my hands, and I said, "What do you want to do?"

T.J. said, "One test is enough to deal with, okay?"

"Test! T.J.!" I said, falling back on the couch.

Couldn't he see me? Was he blind? I was sitting there struggling just like he was.

246

I said, "I'm here with you and I'm hurting and worried and confused and in a few minutes that little piece of plastic is going to determine whether or not we have a permanent tie to each other for life!

"For life!" I said. "This is not a moral issue right now! I'm dealing with the hard facts of everyday life and what it means for two people, who may not want to, to have to deal with each other for the rest of their lives! For two people to have to get together and be responsible and care for a kid. That's what I'm talking about!"

sixty-eight
t.j.

"I know that!" I shouted back at Sandy. "I know what I have to do and if you're pregnant I will take care of our child. A man takes care of what's his and I know that baby would be mine. My daddy has always taken care of me, been a father to me. What right would I have if we decided to have a child to walk out and leave it? Hell no, that's not what a Willet man does."

I told Sandy, "Willet men take care of their children, so if you're pregnant and we decide to have it I will take care of my child."

Sandy said, "My? Willet men? You're talking from the head and not the heart."

I don't know where I was talking from, but did it matter if I was going to do the right thing?

I said, "Sandy, it don't matter head or heart—just to do the right thing is what matters."

Sandy gave me a half-smile and it wasn't one of being pleased or amused or anything that I could put my finger on.

Then her eyebrows raised and she said, "Look!"

I held my breath and glanced down.

sandy

Blue! Blue! I never even liked blue that much until this moment! I wasn't pregnant. T.J. looked up at me and smiled. We both jumped up and hugged. We hugged and hugged and hugged. I felt something pass between us. The hug felt good and necessary and I didn't want to let go even though I felt it. A loss? Something was missing and maybe if we hugged longer it would come back. But I knew that it was gone. How? Maybe it was the stress of all that had happened. Maybe we just needed a little time to pass between us until the juices settled. But I knew it. I looked in T.J.'s eyes and I could tell he knew it too. He touched my lip with his index finger and flicked away a chip of polish that had been on my lip.

"Oh," I said, because I knew nothing else to say.

T.J. played with my bottom lip for a minute, then he said, "I'll call you."

I nodded okay and even added, "Sure."

I watched him pick up his coat and walk out the door and he looked back once or twice and I even winked at him. After the door shut, my tears came rolling free-fall.

speed

Two things T.J. got from his mama. One is his good hair and the other is his talent for holding a grudge. That boy can hold a grudge tighter than a bum holds a begging cup. Yep-yep-yep! Swear ta God. I knew I was going to hurt him when I told him about me and Ann having an affair while I was married to his mama. Knew that. But deep down I felt he would understand and be able to come to me with that hurt. But T.J. would rather stew about it than bring it to me. I know we are gonna clash but I know there's one saving grace.

Ya see, there's this thing, not a wall or barrier or hurdle but maybe the best word for it would be a breaker. I think fathers and sons have a breaker between them to catch hold of the different tides in their lives. I can remember my daddy and me going at odds over little things, like curfews and clothes and lingo. Anger and confusion and misunderstanding and yelling and chest beating. All that went on but it's natural. There are things that go on between a father and son, bonding that takes place from learning how to make a level bat swing or explaining that first hard-on and all other kinds of things like that. The knowledge that sails from cap to cap is real, but as boys grow into men they want to challenge their fathers. They want to see if they got the hardtop that the old man has . . . if their engine is as sharp as his. And fathers get pissed when the boy comes at him like that but he knows the boy is coming. He's got to try you, and all fathers can accept this. The breaker is what keeps the two from crashing into each other. That breaker is respect. It's love. It's fear.

Now, T.J. has idolized me so and I have to tell the truth, put my hand over my heart, and tell the story that I've been eatin' that up. As a black man in America it's a rare and beautiful thing to be put on a pedestal. Don't care who puts you there! If you get up there as a black man, it feels so good that you just don't never, ever want to come down. Now, of course that pedestal is not in world view, it's in the eye of the beholder. 'Cause the world kicks a black man's ass like clockwork. Every chance the world gets, its boot heel is swinging toward a black man's back pocket. It's as simple as that. It's as simple and hurtful as people looking at you like you're dirt and clutching their pocketbooks to not getting that job promotion that you should have. Women get discriminated against too but it's not the same because a man is supposed to take the lead in the world.

So T.J. put me on a pedestal and I dug the hell out of it. He never, ever really challenged me because he had me up so very, very high. He idolized me so much and for so long that I even stopped worrying about fallin' off. I figured there was no wrong that I could do in my son's eyes that he could not accept or understand. Now I wonder, could I have been wrong? Did I let his idolizing blind me to the fact that T.J., not like a son but like a human being, can be hard? I need so much for that breaker, that breaker between fathers and sons, to hold for me and T.J.

He didn't come visit me in the hospital but he did call. And the day I checked out, Outlaw came and got me.

Outlaw said, "If I was a man with a son and we was having a falling-out, I wouldn't let it go but so far before I stopped it."

That's the way Outlaw gives advice—he feeds it through his imaginary self. But he's talking about you. Outlaw knows it. And you know it. This was advice I appreciated but advice that I had already given myself.

I went home and got settled in. I was like Dorothy in *The Wiz*, ain't no place like home. I was tired of that stiff, lumpy hospital bed and that hard water that hardly made you feel wet after taking a shower. I unpacked my little bag and threw my pajamas in the hamper and put up the medicine the doctor gave me. I went to the icebox and threw out two bottles of hot sauce, a package of neck bones, some leftover chitterlings, and I got the last can of beer and sipped it slow. One step at a time, I can't run before I walk. I finished the beer.

Then I took the phone off the hook and watched TV and then went to sleep. I didn't wake up until the next morning. I stayed in bed for two days, no phone or nothing, and slept solid. Then one night I staggered into a ragged sleep. Torn around the edges and nary a bit of comfort at all, that kind of sleep. The problem was that my mind wanted to stay alert and worry about T.J. but my body was begging for the familiar rest it got from my broken-in mattress and my extra-firm pillows. That kind of tug-of-war was bound to set off something ugly. And that something was my dream. Sometimes you can't remember your dreams exactly but you'll wake up with a real uneasy feeling or a real happy feeling. Either way, doggoned if you don't want to remember that dream. Yep-yep-yep! I had a rare experience for me. I remembered my dream completely. I mean every detail. It felt so real too!

I was standing by a set of train tracks in the desert somewhere. There was nothing but sand all around me. Tracks and sand. I was standing there with a sledgehammer resting against my hip, dungarees on, a bandanna on my head, and sweat pouring down my bare back. In the distance I heard the *thung-thung-cha* of the train. I couldn't see it. But I could hear it. I looked up at the sun—all flat, red, and blistering in the sky. It was so hot! I looked down at the rail in front of me and it was crooked. It was bent up like a Z. A big zag, you dig? Picture what I'm saying. I'm seeing the rail and I hear *thung-thung-cha!* The train is coming. My eyes followed that bent-up track and I can't seem to take my eyes off of it even though I'm beginning to hear something else. That something else is a piano.

It's T.J. playing, see? He's going *bee-bop-tha-dah*. I can't see him but I can hear and feel him. I know my child. And my son, my son is playing his mama's song. The song he played that last time Shine was deathbed sick. My eyes followed that track and finally I did lay vision on him sitting at his grandma's big upright piano. The piano straddled the train tracks. *Bee-bop-tha-dah*. Now the train is coming. It's getting closer. Then it hit me. That Z? That zag? Is putting that train on a collision course right for T.J. I yelled, "Get outta the way, fool!" T.J. just kept on playing. I yelled, "Move, Negro!" He went right on playing.

I started swinging that sledgehammer. I know I've gotta slam that rail straight to save my boy. *Pow-pow!* I'm pounding out that zag. I'm hearing *thung-thung-cha . . . bee-bop-tha-dah . . . pow-pow!* My hands are hurting. My legs are hurting. My chest is hurting. I feel my heart swelling. And the rail is barely budging and I can feel tears rolling down my face. I'm pounding and pounding that rail. *Pow-pow.* And I stop and wipe my hands on the sides of my pants to get a better grip. And when I reach back, there's two sets of hands on the hammer. I recognized the extra-large knuckles, the coloring, and the scars. Daddy's hands. Now we're swinging together. I see only our hands and I feel Daddy. And the rail is moving and the train is coming and we're swinging. Then the train roars through. I see the steel wheels coming and they cut the hammer into splinters and the force knocks me flat. The hot sand is all across my shoulder blades and I'm looking up at the cherry-red swirls that are the sun and I can't breathe. And what do I hear? *Bee-bop-tha-dah!* And look like then and only then can I dare to take a breath. And when I do? I wake up. I got up and I got dressed. I went over to T.J.'s place.

When I stepped on the porch, I was thinking about what I was going to say. And it wasn't until I had my key in the door and a flicker of snow caught my eye that I got a chill. The chill was from the memory of being laid out on this porch, helpless. I felt a flush of heat run through me next and that is a weird feeling to run cold then hot like that but I did. And I took it. I stood for a minute and took a couple of deep breaths. Then the whole feeling left me. Bye-bye. Gone. I put the key in and went in.

I went for T.J.'s bedroom, which used to be Mama and Daddy's room, and dogged if I didn't feel like a kid again on those old stairs. I remember sneaking up those steps to keep Mama and Daddy from hearing me come in too late. If I remembered, and I did, if you stepped in the corners nearest the base of the stairs it didn't creak as loud. I walked up slowly and went into T.J.'s bedroom.

He was wrapped up in steel-gray sheets with his arm slung across his eyes, lightly snoring. I watched him for a moment and wished wings on his dreams so they could help carry him through life.

There was Mama's rocker by the dresser and I sat down in it and there, right there, was a picture of Shine. That old picture showed Shine sitting on our back porch smiling, holding a wicker basket of white sheets and wearing a pink top and a red apron, and behind her the sun is rising, throwing light over her shoulder like a shawl and the empty, roped clotheslines are drawing stripes beyond her arms. They framed Shine like a picture. It's tough to miss somebody. A bare spot is tough to cover, I swear. I sat in that rocker and thought about our dances, our kisses, our joy at birth, our fears of the illness that just caught us like beetle bugs in a web. I thought about my choices and my decisions.

And that's when I heard T.J. say, "Daddy!"

He was sweating. "Daddy, you scared me! What's the matter with you?" he shouted as he leaned forward half out of bed and half in.

I didn't say anything to him. He reached for the lamp but stopped because there was enough daylight in the room. He saw something in my face, I imagine, and that brought his hand and his eyes down.

T.J. started explaining, "Sorry I didn't pick you up and haven't called. I got tied up with some things with Sandy and I just . . ."

I didn't want to hear that. I said, "Be a man."

T.J. said, "What?"

I told him again. "Be a man," I said. "You've got a bone to pick with me—so pick it." And I started to rock in that chair. I had my hands folded across my lap just as calm and cool, rocking. I said, "You're mad, so say it."

T.J. looked away, shrugged, scratched his chest. "Daddy," he said, "I don't feel like going into this."

Did I ask him what he felt like doing?

I said, "I don't care about your mood this morning, son, really I don't." He had a gripe with me. "You want a piece of me, T.J.," I said. "I can see it in your eyes, you want a piece of me."

T.J. still wouldn't look at me, but he said, "Why are you barging into my place unannounced and trying to start trouble, huh?"

"I got something to deal with," I told him, "and I want to kick it to the curb right now." We had trouble to deal with. I said, "Boy, you are hurt and if you don't get it out it's going to lay deep inside of you and grow and get fat and sassy and ugly and sneaky like an el rat and I don't want that. I told you about what happened because I needed to come clean and I needed to face some things. That's what a man does. I'm off the pedestal I know. I'm not solid gold in your eyes no more. But that's okay 'cause I had a damn good run but what I want to know is did I just fall or did I crumble? Huh, son, did old Speed fall or did he crumble?"

t.j.

When I saw Daddy, I wanted to tell him how hurt and disappointed I was at him but I was worried about his heart.

I said, "Daddy, the doctor said . . ."

He said, "Fuck the doctor! This is you and me, boy. Ain't no doctor here."

Then he got up and sat on the side of my bed. Daddy popped my chest with the back of his hand and said, "What's up?"

I bit my lip. He popped me again. I blurted out so hard and loud that I could see my own spit, "What were you fucking around on her for? Huh? Man, you told me all this stuff about how much you loved her and that she was the only woman for you and one day I'd find a woman like that. But hell, you stepped out on her, and that means there is no loyalty in the world to no one or nobody. I'm not being a baby about it but I'm pissed and I know that you were wrong and you know it 'cause you wouldn't have said anything if you didn't. Now, how am I suppose to feel? How am I suppose to conduct myself now that you took one of the most precious memories of mine away?"

"Son, son!" Daddy said.

"No! You've got me confused and I didn't need that. Life is hard enough. Being out in the world is hard enough. Finding love and loving is hard enough, Daddy, without you throwing me a knuckleball. What's up with that? Was that all you were thinking

256

about when she was sick? When her mind was unraveling at the seams, you were thinking about Miss Ann? What's up with that, Daddy? Whatcha, whatcha want me to do with that info, huh? I put you on a pedestal and now you fell. Hell, you jumped off, if anything."

seventy-two

speed

"Boy," I told him, "life changes and people change. Mistakes are made."

T.J. said, "I know that."

"Well, act like it then," I said. I popped him in the chest and I said, "People will disappoint you in life and that's not a reason to damn them to hell. People are not God or godlike. When they get lucky, they can find their way in the goodness that we all want to have. But you are going to step out of bounds sometimes. Sometimes it matters and other times it doesn't. I made a mistake and I wanted and needed to share it with you because I didn't want you to do the same things. I didn't want you to step in every puddle I did. That's all. I'm a father trying to help his son is all. I don't need your forgiveness because I didn't do anything to you."

T.J. turned his head then. I grabbed his collar and shook him. "Boy, I need your understanding and I need you to see me man-to-man on this and accept that I can err. That's what I'm talking about here. This ain't no home remedy. Your hurt will be there for a while and then it will go away, but what I don't want to go away is what we have that is special between us. Talk to me, T.J. Talk to me."

t.j.

Daddy scared me. I could feel us going at it. I was scared for myself. I love my old man so much and I want him to be every-thing to me and that is a mistake, I think. Sitting there listening to him, I realized that I made a mistake. I want everything and I'm just not going to get everything I want from everybody. Pe-riod.

I said, "Daddy, you know I just wanted everything from you and I put too much of a demand on us—on what we have. Last night Sandy thought she was pregnant and for a while I thought I was going to be a father and it was overwhelming. I'm not saying that I'm not mad and I'm not saying that I understand, but I'm saying that I realize from that little bit and from everything that you're saying and I'm feeling that there are no rules in life. We've got to take relationships and their twists and turns as they come and not wallow in it, but accept and move on. That's what I'm feeling now, Daddy. I love you and I'm still hurting but I can accept it and move on."

Daddy didn't say anything and he didn't smile but he looked satisfied and he held out his hand and I shook it. I made sure that my eyes never left his, then I brought him to me and we hugged for a long time.

seventy-four

bebe

I asked Sandy, "You heard from T.J.?"

Several weeks had gone by and Sandy said they had dinner once but nothing was happening really. She looked a little sad and I think it's because Sandy has a hard time of letting go. We all do a bit, I guess. To let go means you're dismissing the need. And everybody likes to hold on to their needs because they keep good company. But as time kept on, her spirits lifted, particularly when my graduation week came up.

I made it! There were times when I thought that I was going to mess up. I thought I wasn't going to make it but I did. I was so proud of myself! Get down, yeah! I had all my credits lined up. I could have waited for the spring graduation but I opted for the winter ceremony. I was not "ready" but "reat" to get my diploma. I couldn't sleep the night before. I tossed and turned and I woke up in the middle of the night. And the sky looked so dark and pretty and shiny. I felt like it was shining just for me. I started imagining my name being called over and over and over again. I had such a feeling of accomplishment. I wished my mother was alive to see it. She would be so proud. I was proud enough for the both of us.

Now that I'd have my degree, I'd been thinking about other jobs I could apply for. With my bank experience, I could maybe move up there or go to another company. I had more possibilities. More opportunities. I wished that I had done this earlier but you can't rotate a clock backwards and why try? Every experience is something to build on, a block taking you somewhere, so hey! I was so glad Sandy bugged me into doing it.

The morning of my graduation my hair looked great. Child, I was on my fourth hairdresser in this never-ending battle to have hallelujah hair—hair that's good and glorious. I put on the new dress I bought. It was creme and I had this elegant necklace and earrings that I'd spent one entire paycheck on. So ya know it was real, huh? Sandy came by to pick me up and she brought me a corsage of pink, purple, and white flowers and there was a little ribbon tied to it that said, "Graduate." Ain't my girl cool? I gave her a big hug. Sandy looked dignified as always and I had my robe and cap in my hand.

Sandy said, "Put it on!"

And I slipped the robe on and pranced around kicking up my heels.

And Sandy said, "The cap too!"

"Oh, no! My hair is looking too good, okay? No telling when it will look this good again," I told her.

Sandy laughed when I said that.

We got to the auditorium and it was crowded. I didn't realize that there were so many people in my class. There was a boom of excitement in the air. Most of my classmates were younger. I envied them even now with the weight of experience on my side. There's something wonderful about having seasons and selections ahead of you when you are young enough to believe every pick is a sure thing.

I found my place backstage. I marched with my head held high and I looked out into the balcony at all the faces. I found my family in a row on the main floor, up close. My cousins were there, my great-aunt and -uncle, and Sandy. She was waving like crazy and smiling just about as hard as I was. I nodded dignified and that froze her for a second, then she laughed and started waving again.

I knew what she meant now about how the moment made you stately almost—that was her word, but cool, it fit. I strutted across that stage, not like Patti but like a peacock. Oh yeah, I earned this bad boy and I wanted to let everybody know it. I shook the president's hand, took the scroll, and I held it like it was my scepter. I was ruling this day, okay?

After it was over, we all met out in the lobby at a point that we had designated beforehand. My cousins were cheering and hugging me and my great-aunt was crying and stuff and Sandy was grinning and my universe was feeling absolutely perfect. Then I felt this hand, very firm, pressed in the middle of my back to turn me. I looked around and there was this fine, do you hear me, fine man standing in front of me. He was six four with broad shoulders and a barrel chest. He looked like he was oh, about forty to forty-five years old and he had a sexy little gap in his front teeth. He was steak brown with smooth skin and a little hair on his chin.

I said, "Hello."

He said, "Excuse me, I just wanted to congratulate you on getting your degree."

I said thank you and then he went on to say his name was Isaac and that he was attending his friend's graduation. I didn't know his friend but I sure was glad to know him. I had new picks and choices ahead of me.

Isaac said, "Would you like to go out sometime?"

Would I? Sandy looked at me out of the corner of her eye and winked.

I told Isaac, "The pleasure would be all mine."

My sabbatical came to an end right there in my mind. I wasn't jumping to conclusions but I was ready to get back out there. I wasn't sure where this chance meeting was going to go, but I was glad to be moving into a new phase of possibilities. And isn't that what life is all about?